THE
GOLDEN AGE
OF
MONTAUK
SPORTFISHING

INTERVIEWS WITH
EIGHT LEGENDARY CAPTAINS

BILL AKIN

PREFACE BY JOE GAVIOLA

The Golden Age of Montauk Sportfishing:
Interviews with Eight Legendary Captains

Published by WDA Publishing

Copyright © 2021 by Bill Akin

Second printing July 2021

All rights reserved

978-1-7370314-0-6

PHOTO CREDITS

Front cover: unknown

Back cover portrait: Grant Monahan

akinauthor.com

CONTENTS

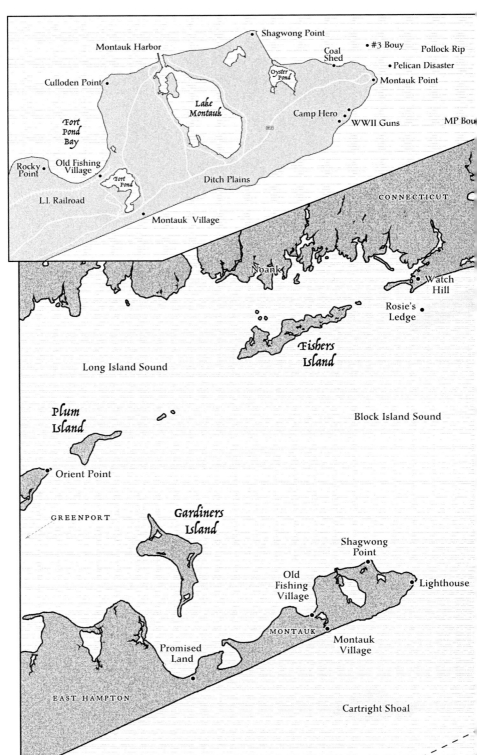

Shagwong Point

Montauk Harbor

Coal Shed

#3 Bouy   Pollock Rip

Pelican Disaster

Culloden Point

Oyster Pond

Montauk Point

Fort Pond Bay

Lake Montauk

Camp Hero

WWII Guns

MP Bou

Rocky Point

Old Fishing Village

Fort Pond

Ditch Plains

L.I. Railroad

Montauk Village

CONNECTICUT

Noank

Watch Hill

Rosie's Ledge

Fishers Island

Long Island Sound

Plum Island

Block Island Sound

Orient Point

GREENPORT

Gardiners Island

Shagwong Point

Old Fishing Village

Lighthouse

MONTAUK

Montauk Village

Promised Land

EAST HAMPTON

Cartright Shoal

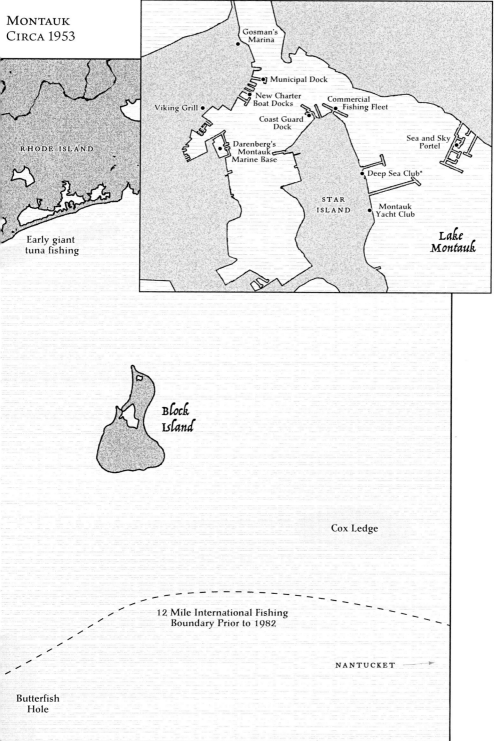

MONTAUK
CIRCA 1953

RHODE ISLAND

Early giant
tuna fishing

Gosman's
Marina

Municipal Dock

New Charter
Boat Docks

Viking Grill

Commercial
Fishing Fleet

Coast Guard
Dock

Darenberg's
Montauk
Marine Base

Sea and Sky
Portel

Deep Sea Club*

STAR
ISLAND

Montauk
Yacht Club

Lake
Montauk

Block
Island

Cox Ledge

12 Mile International Fishing
Boundary Prior to 1982

NANTUCKET

Butterfish
Hole

* est. 1960

v

DEDICATION

This book is dedicated to Captains – past, present, and future.
They guide us out on the ocean and bring us safely home.
Each time our lives are in their hands.

The Viking Grill in the late 1960s.

PREFACE

THE DISTANCE BETWEEN THE MONTAUK YACHT CLUB AND THE VIKING Grill, both located in Montauk Harbor, was not much more than a couple of long surfcasting flings. While the cuisine and clientele in the 1950s, '60s, and '70s differed, the soul of each place was the professional captains and mates, working fishermen. They ran charter boats out of the docks near the Viking Grill and private boats from the Yacht Club.

As a teenager in the late 1960s, I worked nights as a busboy at the Yacht Club. I would follow up my shift with a 4 AM breakfast at the Viking Grill and then a full day of fishing. Breakfast choices at the Grill included eggs with either bacon, sausage, or ham. That was it. The floor was warped linoleum and if you were lucky, you might get a stool at the counter. Most men smoked, and the ceiling had a brown tint. The fish mounts on the wall were crinkled with age. It was always loud, smoky, and full of energy.

The captains held center stage whenever they spoke. And the one thing the captains liked to do as much as fish was to talk about fishing. Just sitting there among these veterans was intimidating for me as a teenager.

Decades later, the Viking Grill was transformed into a famous high-end restaurant (Dave's Grill), one of my all-time favorites. But even then when I sat at the bar, I couldn't help thinking back to those early morning breakfasts. The excitement, the stories, the scent of fish scales from pants and shirts that would never know clean, even the smoke. I still miss every minute of it.

The Montauk Yacht Club was like working on another planet. The Viking Grill and nearby docks smelled like clams but at the Yacht Club there were fresh flowers, starched uniforms, and men in blue blazers. The pace was more deliberate, formality a requirement, and traditions respected. For me, though, whether it was the Yacht Club, the charter boat docks, or the

Viking Grill, it was always the professionals, the captains, who stood out.

Most wore khaki pants, topsiders, captain hats, and blue jackets to block the wind. When they took their caps off there was always a tan line that stopped right above the nose revealing a white forehead extending up to whatever hairline might still exist. Creases generated by decades of staring across miles of ocean coursed out from the corner of each man's eyes. Their hands were working man hands, scarred and bruised from decades of cutting bait, tying knots, twisting wire, and gaffing fish.

I worked as a mate on several charter boats from the late '60s through the '70s. Fishing was so much a passion for me that I commuted back from college in Rhode Island on weekends. It was serious work, and every captain was on you in a second if you weren't at your best. It was their livelihood and reputation. Every fish counted, and just like in the movies, the captain was well ...THE CAPTAIN. And for me, the pay was great. Heading back to college with $200 cash in my pocket after just a weekend, I felt like a Rockefeller (maybe not quite).

I had no way to know then, but those years were the tail end of the golden age of sportfishing chronicled in this book. The fishing was spectacular and the days exhausting for both captains and mates. I know those seasons were long, June through November, but they went by in a flash.

After years in the corporate world, I moved back to Montauk with my family and started a small group of local businesses. The most popular was Gaviola's Montauk Market. I opened it in 1988 right in the middle of the Montauk Harbor area. By then there were dinner restaurants, gift stores, and still one or two places open for breakfast. But no place to buy food. Montauk had never had a full-service market that catered to fishermen.

I opened the store at 5 AM every day, 364 days a year. I was open three hours before anyone else. Gaviola's Montauk Market became the epicenter of morning fishing activity. Almost every captain, mate, and fisherman (and fisherwoman) started their day dropping by for coffee, an egg sandwich, or something for lunch. While we prepped the kitchen, I left the back door open for any captain or mate who had to leave the dock before 5 AM. They could help themselves and settle up later. And they always did!

Over the years I had the market (1988-2015), the captains depicted in *The Golden Age of Montauk Sportfishing* were at or near the end of their careers. But each one still came in almost every day to talk with the new generation about fish, fishing, and some of their more memorable charters.

My favorite days were those when it was too rough to leave the dock or early mornings during the offseason. Sometimes the talk went on all day. Bob Tuma and Harry Clemenz might hold court for an hour only to be joined by Ralph Pitts or Paul Forsberg. The stories were priceless.

These men were the pioneers of a fledgling industry that turned Montauk into the Fishing Capital of the World. Bill Akin and I were exceptionally fortunate to know many of them well enough for them to accept our invitation to sit down one morning at the old Tipperary Inn. We listened quietly for more than two hours as these captains, most in their 80s, shared childhood memories, talked about days when they caught swordfish and giant bluefin tuna just a few miles off the beach, and why the fishing we have today is a mere shadow of what they saw.

I believe what Bill has pulled together in *The Golden Age* is the foremost history of Montauk sportfishing told by men who lived it. I feel blessed to have known these men. Each one meant a great deal to me, and I know they will always mean a great deal to Montauk. Here, in their own words, are their stories.

Joe Gaviola
February 2021

Frank (left) and Bob Tuma circa 1946 ©Montauk Library. Dave Edwardes Collection

INTRODUCTION

IN JUNE 1994, A GROUP OF SIX VETERAN MONTAUK CAPTAINS, ALL longtime friends, gathered around a table at the Tipperary Inn near the center of Montauk Harbor. Their faces were all permanently tanned, rutted, and scorched, evidence of lives lived on the ocean. For hours they laughed, told fish stories, remembered some of their best days fishing, and shared a few solemn moments. As witnesses to both the good and bad, they did not hesitate to criticize actions they thought had hurt the fishing in Montauk. All had been on the water the day the *Pelican* capsized, drowning forty-five souls, and each had played a major role as Montauk was transformed from an obscure commercial fishing port into a world-renowned sportfishing destination.

My friend Joe Gaviola and I had, from time to time, enjoyed hearing each of these men tell some of their stories, but we realized it might be even more fun if we could get them to sit down face to face to see what developed. We were not disappointed.

Around the table at the Tipperary that day were Ralph Pitts, Frank Tuma, Bob Tuma, Carl Darenberg, George Potts, and Harry Clemenz. Later that year I recorded Gus Pitts at his home on Shepherd's Neck, and finally, Joe and I recorded Paul Forsberg in December, 2019 in an apartment above the Montauk Lighthouse Museum..

While this book focuses on the times these men recalled from their fishing days, each of them, and their wives, contributed in many important ways as members of the Montauk community.

No doubt there are many captains still working today who could add their own memories to what follows. Montauk's fishing history deserves a more comprehensive look that includes not only an updated review of Montauk sportfishing but also the story of Montauk surfcasting, local baymen, and the all-important commercial fishing industry. A much bigger book for sure.

Nevertheless, that morning in June '94 the intention was simply to capture, in their own words, what these legendary captains had to say. Only when a ninety-one-page transcript of the tapes turned up twenty-five years later did Joe and I realize what a treasure we had recorded with this collection of first hand testimonies.

The careers of these eight captains spanned the decades of the 1950s, '60s, and '70s when white marlin were plentiful, swordfish were caught only a few miles from the beach, giant bluefin tuna migrated through Block Island Sound every September, and sharks were so common that few boats even considered fishing for them. It was also an age when the notion of an angler profiting from a catch was never a consideration. It was an age of fishing only for sport, Montauk's golden age of sportfishing.

The Captains

Bob (1922 – 2008) and **Frank Tuma** (1924 – 2018) were cousins. Their fathers, Charlie and Frank Tuma, Sr., moved to Montauk in the early 1920s. Together they started fishing as lobstermen, and progressed into commercial trawling. Running out of Fort Pond Bay, Charlie Tuma was the first to convert his boat to charter fishing. Bob Tuma ran the charter boat *Dawn* for decades while cousin Frank Jr. also ran charters until switching to a career in retail sales and real estate.

Carl Darenberg (1925 – 2009) arrived in Montauk in 1932 from Freeport, Long Island. His father, Carl Sr., worked for Gus Pitts and then, with Carl Jr. as his mate, he began running charters on his boat, the *Foretenate*, out of the Montauk Yacht Club in 1936. The Darenbergs were one of the first fishermen to move to Florida for the winters where they met some of the early pioneers of sportfishing. Carl also picked up a few techniques in Florida he later introduced to Montauk such as the use of wire lines.

Harry Clemenz (1931 – 2015) was born in Elmhurst, Queens, and would camp with his parents all summer at Hither Hills in the 1940s. The family moved to Montauk toward the end of that decade when his parents bought a small rooming house next to what is now the ballfield. His father began running the charter boat *Ginger* from the Fishangri-La dock with young Harry as his mate. By 1960, Harry had transitioned to running private boats in Montauk, Florida, and the Bahamas. Running out of Montauk and often working without a mate, Harry ran the *Doc's In* and the *Nassau Miss* and still produced one successful season after another. Again working without a mate in 1986, Harry caught the biggest blue marlin (1,174 pounds) ever landed in Montauk.

Ralph Pitts (1917 – 1995) was born in Noank, Connecticut, and arrived in Montauk when he was about nine years old. His family was originally from Nova Scotia. Ralph's father was a commercial fisherman and had been making spring and summer trips across the sound to Montauk before he decided to bring the family over permanently. Ralph fished with his father for years and then operated four of his own boats all named after his wife and business partner, Margaret. Ralph was also a founding member of the Montauk Fire Department and Fire Chief for two separate terms. He retired from charter fishing in 1976 but continued to run the private boat *Shady Lady* in Montauk and *Eleuthera* until his death.

George Potts (1914 – 2000) and his brother, **John** (1921 – 1984), started running a charter boat in 1944 out of Freeport, Long Island. They soon began making trips to Montauk, and after a few years relocated both their home and business. George and John were both licensed captains, but most days George ran the boat while John managed the cockpit as the mate. Their first boat was called the *Tuna* followed early on by the *Bluefin*, and then, without interruption, by the *Bluefin IV* run by George's son, Capt. Michael Potts. Both George Potts and his wife, Margaret, were pilots with Margaret often flying offshore to spot swordfish for the boat.

Gus Pitts (1907 – 1998) was born in Nova Scotia and came to Montauk when he was seven years old. He first worked as a trap fish-erman with his father and later the two ran a commercial boat together. Gus eventually ran his own charter boats *Marie, Marie II,* and *Marie III* until he retired in 1974. Gus also managed to fit in a short but dramatic stint as a bootlegger.

Paul Forsberg (1939) was twelve years old when he came to Montauk in 1951 from Freeport with his mother and father. For several years he helped his father run the *Viking V* as a party boat and later as a charter boat. Paul began the expansion of the Viking fleet with the *Viking Starlight* and later the *Viking Star.* The modern Viking fleet consists of seven vessels.

A Young Carl Darenberg (left) and his father (far right) circa 1946. ©Montauk Library. Dave Edwardes Collection

THE EARLY DAYS

The fishermen know the sea is dangerous
and the storm terrible, but they have never found
these dangers sufficient reason for remaining ashore.

VINCENT VAN GOGH

Fisher's crew digs through the dunes to open Lake Montauk to Block Island Sound. Circa 1927

A HOLE IN
THE DUNES

That fish launched a future no one saw coming.

BILL AKIN

IT TOOK A HORSE-DRAWN PLOUGH, A FEW MEN WITH SHOVELS, AND some dynamite to prepare Montauk for what lay ahead.

Miami Beach developer Carl Fisher knew Montauk could never meet his ambitious expectations without a protected harbor. So in 1927 he ordered his crew to dig a trench through a narrow strand of dunes to connect Montauk's fresh-water Great Pond with Block Island Sound. In just a few days the biggest freshwater lake on Long Island was transformed into a saltwater estuary. That act, unimaginable under current environmental laws, resulted in Lake Montauk, three miles from Montauk Point, now one of the finest ports on the East Coast, and home to over a thousand boats.

Opening Montauk Harbor created potential, but real change was still decades away. It took a hurricane, the Navy, a maritime tragedy, and one big fish to set the future in motion.

Before 1927, and despite its extreme exposure to northerly winds, Fort Pond Bay was home port for Montauk's fishermen. It was also the location of Montauk village, the post office, and the rail depot where fish were shipped to New York. With Fort Pond Bay as action central, fishermen were in no rush to move their boats to the new protected docks at Fisher's recently completed Montauk Yacht Club. While an elegant architectural testimony to his grand vision, only a skeleton fleet of private yachts and a few charter boats elected to tie up there. The Yacht Club catered to an elite social crowd, not Montauk's predominantly commercial fleet, or the thousands of blue-collar fishermen who arrived weekends onboard the Fisherman's Special train at Fort Pond Bay.

In the thirteen years between 1938 and 1951 a series of events changed everything. The '38 hurricane demolished many of the Fort Pond Bay homes and docks. Then with World War II the U.S. Navy appropriated the entire area, paying locals $300 to move whatever homes remained or had been rebuilt. When the Navy moved out after the war, boats resumed fishing from the docks left behind.

Then in 1951 the overloaded fishing boat, *Pelican*, capsized coming around Montauk Point when a sudden nor'easter surprised the fleet on Labor Day weekend. Forty-five people, including the captain, were lost. Lawsuits followed. One suit named the Long Island Rail Road as responsible, saying its Fishermen's Special train encouraged an excessive number of fishermen to come to Montauk. Soon thereafter the LIRR canceled the Fisherman's Special, and the boats that serviced the fishermen who depended on the train finally relocated to Montauk Harbor.

Two years before the *Pelican* tragedy, Kay Topping, the petite wife of New York Yankees owner Dan Topping, landed the first giant bluefin tuna brought into Montauk. That fish launched a future no one saw coming.

SO YOU THINK YOU'RE A LOCAL

The traveling then was by horse when we first started.
There were eleven of us: six girls, two boys,
my mother and father, and a friend.

GUS PITTS

MANY OF THE FAMILIES WHO WERE A PART OF MONTAUK'S EVOLUTION from obscurity into a major fishing destination arrived decades before changes began to accelerate. For the most part they lived in what today would be considered wooden shacks. These crude homes put up between the railroad tracks and Fort Pond Bay on the north side of the Montauk peninsula provided easy access to the fishing boats docked or moored on stakes just off the beach. There was no indoor plumbing, only wood stoves for heat and cooking and kerosene lamps or candles for light. And this was year-round. In winter, eight-inch blocks of ice were cut from Fort Pond and Tuthill Pond, stored in local ice houses insulated with layers of straw, and used year-round for shipping fish by train to New York. It was not an easy life, but many of these first families had come down from Nova Scotia or Newfoundland — Montauk winters were an improvement.

The story of the extensive Pitts family, Gus and cousin Ralph among them, is typical of how many of the early families found their way to Montauk. This is what Gus Pitts recalled of his family's journey: *We came to Montauk in 1914. On July 26, we landed in Montauk from Nova Scotia. The traveling then was by horse when we first started. There were eleven of us: six girls, two boys, my mother and father, and a friend.*

The first lap was by horse and wagon. Then we crossed by ferry where the guy had to push the ferry across. Then the second lap, we took the train to Halifax, and then we stayed in Shore Oak overnight. We took the train that morning and landed in Yarmouth. We stayed there overnight. Then we took the boat the next morning for Boston. We were on it all night. We got to North Station in Boston the next morning where we transferred by horse and wagon to South Station. Then we took another train to Connecticut. That's where my father took us to Montauk on his twenty-two-foot boat. We crossed the Sound with all the baggage and the crew.

The Napeague Promised Land Fish Factory was operating at the time with four bunker boats: the *Amagansett*, the *East End*, the *Ocean View*, and the *Elizabeth*. Management realized that the Canadians they had working for them were more reliable than any other crew they were able to hire. They put the word out.

Gus Pitts: *I think they hired some sixty something men from Nova Scotia. They had their own bunkhouse on Promised Land, and their own cook-house.*

My father worked on those boats for seven years, and then he went into business for himself. He bought a little dragger. Then I started working for my father when I was seventeen.

After a couple of years fishing in the bay, Gus and his father "got a little more nerve up and we went outside to drag on the ocean side, that's where the fish were — fluke, they weren't fluke, they were doormats, fourteen to sixteen pounds. The little ones, four pounds, we would throw away."

Ralph Pitts, Gus's cousin, came over from Noank, Connecticut, around 1920. He was the only one of the original Pitts family not born in Nova Scotia. Before Ralph came to Montauk, his father and uncle, along with Tom Joyce and Sam Joyce, would bring their boats over to Montauk from Connecticut in the spring. They anchored their small draggers near Oyster Pond and lived in the building that was used to store coal for the lighthouse in winter. There was enough room for the four men to shelter, but only in the spring after most of the coal had been burned up.

Ralph's father would fish for cod using setlines: *I was only a kid, and we lived in the fishing village. He and others had sea skiffs, Jersey skiffs. They'd haul them up on the beach at night. They'd bait their trolls and the next morning they'd put them in the water. They set the gear off Culloden. There'd be a cod fish on every second or third hook. As soon as you set the gear, you'd go to the other end and start hauling it. Sometimes you'd wait an hour before you started hauling back. There were a lot of fish around here then. A lot of fish.*

A lot of fish for sure. Gus remembered other local fishermen, or baymen, who made a living using only fish traps similar to the ones you can see today along the beach in Fort Pond Bay. In those days the traps were spread out all the way from North Bar to Gardiners Island.

Gus Pitts: *Joe Clark, Tom Joyce, Dan Parsons, Ernest Parsons, E.B. Tuthill, Frank Parsons, and Ed Thiele all made a living out of thirty-six traps along the bay down to West Point. That was in the twenties. The railroad used to ship anywhere from six carloads of fish a day. Each carload could handle four hundred boxes of fish. That's a lot of fish.*

[The boats in Fort Pond Bay] were anchored on stakes and they had a ringer on the stake. When there was a northeast gale there was so much strain on the stake that they would bend over and the ringer would slip off and the boat would come ashore. So when the wind was over, you'd put them in the water and put them back on the same stake.

For the most part, families came to Montauk to be fishermen. But as Gus discovered seven years after he arrived, there were other ways, albeit short term, to make a living.

TODAY IT WOULD BE CHILD ABUSE

I've been at sea for forty something years and I've never seen anything like this before. Two kids out here on an eighty-five-foot boat with three five hundred horse Liberties, bucking for five hundred cases of liquor.

Captain of a British rumrunner

IMAGINE A FOURTEEN-YEAR-OLD BOY TAKES A WILDLY UNDERPOWERED boat, runs it fifty-five miles offshore, and doesn't come home for a week. And his parents either didn't know he was going, forgot to ask, or possibly encouraged him. If it happened today, the mother and father would probably face child abuse charges, the boy would end up in foster care, and the story would be all over national news. But Gus Pitts was not a modern-day, pampered teenager. At fourteen he already had years of experience on the ocean. What he did in 1921 was not crazy — just maybe a little out of the ordinary.

The story has very little to do with sportfishing, but as Gus tells it, it's just too good to ignore: *My father and I had a twenty-eight-foot dragger with a twelve-horsepower engine.* I started rumrunning with that boat. I used to go fifty-five miles offshore. I was fourteen years old. I'd pick up a hundred cases of liquor. I didn't get in contact with the higher guys, I didn't want to mix it up with those guys. Those guys were tough.*

So I worked with Phil Coffey. He was a regular guy. He used to give me half of a two-dollar bill and the boat had the other half. I had to cross my half with their half. The first time I went out, I found the place where the ship was, but the ship was gone. They had left a smaller sailboat in place. The big boat had left for Block Island. Instead of coming home from fifty-five miles offshore, I headed for Block Island. I found the boat, and I got the load, but I broke down. I was seven days out at sea before I got the engine fixed. I had to fix it myself.

I landed in Connecticut but didn't know where I was. I anchored and swam ashore. Who did I meet but the guy I was working for. He said, "Where the devil have you been? You were supposed to be here seven days ago." I told him I was lost at sea, that my motor broke down, and here I am. They unloaded me, and he threw a cigar box in the boat and told me to give it to Phil Coffey when I got home. I didn't look in the cigar box.

They gave me a bed that night, and breakfast, and enough fuel to get home the next day. The cutter (Coast Guard) was looking for me around nine o'clock because they knew I was out there, but I got in around seven o'clock. I anchored the boat on the mooring. Coffey comes to me and asks me if they gave me a box to bring home? Yeah, I say, it's out there in the boat. Well, he says there's forty-five thousand dollars in that box.

Whoever was running the show must have been impressed. For his next run they gave Gus a slightly bigger boat — eighty-five feet, with a bit more power, three 500-horsepower V-12 Liberty World War I aircraft surplus engines.

Gus Pitts: I used to deliver Culver Cup to Greenport, Shay's Shipyard. It used to take me an hour and a half, Shay's to fifty-five miles offshore. I was capable of making forty-five knots. I picked up a boat called the Eyeson, a big English yacht. I gave them the signal and they put me on a side boom. I climbed up the rope ladder, and the mate looked at me and asked. "Where's the captain?" I said, "I'm the captain." He said, "How old are you?" I told him fifteen. He said, "Well, where's the mate? Bring him up here." The mate's eleven years old. So he brought the two of us up before the captain. He was a big English guy about six foot six. The captain says, "I've been at sea for forty something years and I've never seen anything like this before. Two kids out here on an eighty-five-foot boat with three 500-horse Liberties, bucking for five hundred cases of liquor." They couldn't refuse it because I had the order.

I put on five hundred cases and I got sighted on my way in. They sighted me just off Fort Pond Bay, so I started running for it. They chased me. I drew four and a half feet when the boat was filled, but underway with so much power, the boat rises up and only drew two feet. I cut across the bar inside Gardner's Island, and ran up the creek in Greenport where the Sears and Roebuck is now. I had three rowboats in there with lights, so I knew exactly where to go.

Given his capacity for innovation and risk, it's not hard to see why Gus was destined to become Montauk's best and most creative striped bass fishermen.

*This is how Gus remembers the boat. I suspect that the engine was more powerful as 12 horsepower would not be able to pull even a small dragger net.

In the 1938 hurricane water from Fort Pond Bay swamped the old fishing village. ©Montauk Library, Anne Duryea Kirk scrapbook, Anne Willard Thompson Collection.

’38

*When the women with their children saw the water
coming over the beach, they ran for the train.*

GUS PITTS

THE 1938 HURRICANE WAS THE WORST STORM TO HIT LONG ISLAND IN recorded history. It washed away beach homes from the middle of Long Island out to Montauk and devastated every East End village. People had no warning. Back then there was no system for tracking storms or alerting the public. Even if there had been a warning, it wouldn't have done much good.

As Gus recalled, most people didn't have any idea what a hurricane was: "This guy comes over to our house and tells my wife there's a hurricane coming, Mrs. Pitts. She says, 'Oh let it come.' She didn't know what a hurricane was any more than I did."

The storm raced up the East Coast at an unprecedented speed. Now known as the Long Island Express, it covered the distance from just offshore of Jacksonville, Florida to Long Island in twenty-four hours. The storm was tracking up the coast at sixty-two miles per hour when it slammed into Montauk.

The initial impact was not extreme as the Montauk village and boats were over on the north side at Fort Pond Bay. But when the storm passed by, the wind came around to be directly onshore. The situation deteriorated rapidly.

Gus Pitts: *When the women with their children saw the water coming over the beach, they ran for the train. The track was six feet higher than the beach. They all stayed there through the storm. I jumped in my car and came up*

13

to the bay and rescued my family and my dog. We started for the Montauk Manor and that's where we stayed. Everybody was separated.

The hurricane destroyed most of the houses and the Post Office. Boats were washed up on the beach, but many were relaunched within days. Several of the docks were destroyed. People rebuilt some houses only to have the military arrive three years later and tell them to move. By then the village center had relocated to where it is today, a few feet above sea level and less than three hundred yards from the rising waters of the Atlantic Ocean.

THE FISHERMAN'S SPECIAL

They'd get off the train and go right through the windows. If you
fell down, they'd go right over the top of you, just like cattle.

FRANK TUMA

BEGINNING IN 1932, THE LONG ISLAND RAILROAD operated the Fisherman's Special, a weekend train carrying crowds of eager fishermen to Montauk. The train left Penn Station at four-thirty in the morning, stopped to let a few passengers off in Hampton Bays, then continued to Montauk. The round-trip price for the train, boat trip, and ice was $4.50.

The Fisherman's Special was extremely popular. Arriving in Montauk, passengers struggled to get off to ensure a place on one of the few boats. Riders leaped from the train windows before charging down the dock. Captains were helpless to limit the number of fishermen storming onto their boats. Bob Tuma: "You had a thousand people on that train."

Gus Pitts recalls: "They walked over one guy who had a heart attack. He died on the dock."

Carl Darenberg: *I'm telling you, they would hang out the windows. They wouldn't even wait, they'd jump right out through the windows. They'd be coming down the tracks hanging out the side and if they rolled down the hill they'd be all beat up. All scratched up, jeez they were a mess. We used to call that the Sunday Fun. We'd go down there just to watch them.*

Harry Clemenz recalls, "When you heard that train whistle blow, you got off the dock. You didn't dare stand there."

Frank Tuma: *They'd get off the train and go right through the windows, and they just run. If you fell down, they'd go right over the top of you, just like cattle. It's true. They always told you when you left New York to get on the first boat you come to cause if you didn't you wouldn't get a space.*

Gus Pitts: *They didn't bother to go out the door, they'd crawl out the windows when the train stopped. The rods and their bags, and they'd run for the boats. If the captain didn't stop them and say I've got enough, they'd sink the boat right at the dock. That's how crazy they were.*

Every boat in Montauk's fleet was needed to accommodate the hundreds of would-be fishermen. There wasn't enough space on the small fleet of open, or party, boats. These boats could not accommodate more than about thirty passengers safely. As a result, many fishermen were left with no ride for the day. To fill the demand, local commercial draggers converted their decks and used fish boxes as seats. It didn't matter to the fishermen, they were happy just to get out on the water.

Frank Tuma: *On Sundays the draggers would come over. There were so many people the other boats couldn't take them all. They used to put fish boxes on the deck and turn them upside down and they'd sit on the fish boxes. They didn't have chairs.*

There were a few charter boats mixed in with the draggers and overloaded party boats. To someone arriving for the first time, it was easy to get confused.

Ralph Pitts related one story that happened on his cousin's boat: *This guy's friends had told him that for $2 he got a whole day fishing, but that when he got to Montauk he should run like hell and get on the first boat he* *came to. It just happened that my cousin Gus had the first boat that was at the dock, and just as this guy is jumping aboard, three other guys were also getting on. But these three guys had Gus chartered for the day.*

They started arguing and Gus found it funny that this one guy wasn't talking to the other three. So they got out and started fishing, and they fished the whole day. When they get back to the dock, the guy says to Gus, "What do I owe you?" Gus says, "Thirty-five dollars, the cost for the day's charter." The guy says, "Jeez, I don't want to buy the boat, I just wanted to fish." Gus says, "It's $35 for you and your friends." The guy says, "Friends? I don't even know these guys." It turned out that the three guys didn't say anything because they thought this guy was a friend of Gus, and Gus thought they were all together."

Gus had one of very few charter boats at that time. The main body of the weekend fleet, draggers and open boats, were there for the low-cost train customers. But even with the extra spaces on the draggers, all too often the conventional boats took on far too many passengers. The *Pelican*, a traditional open party boat, was forty-two feet long. She left the dock September 1, 1951 with sixty-four passengers and crew.

At the end of the day fishermen wait on the dock before catching the train back to New York. ©Montauk Library. Al Sari Collection

AFTER THE STORM THE SALVAGE

TOWING LINE is lashed to the bow of the foundered *Pelican* by volunteer Leonard Riley, 19, who swam through rough seas to attach the 3-inch hawser.

GASPING FOR AIR, Diver Tom Innes, state trooper, comes up from cabin where bodies were "all tangled together like a gigantic handful of wrestlers."

HALF-SUNK, the *Pelican* is towed slowly into Montauk Harbor so that a diver can begin his task of finding out how many bodies are trapped inside.

TEMPORARY MORGUE is set up in fishing shack for the ten bodies found on board the *Pelican*. Men leaning over are seeking marks of identification.

FINAL MOORING for the *Pelican* takes place by floodlight at 2:45 Sunday morning. Workers spent rest of night raising boat and bringing out the dead.

FATHER WEEPS helplessly after a Sunday morning visit to fishing shack morgue where he identified the body of his 23-year-old son, Wallace Manko.

The *Pelican* tragedy not only changed the future of Montauk fishing, but also resulted in major upgrades to maritime safety regulation. ©Montauk Library. Sunday Mirror Collection

THE *PELICAN*

He came around the Point and one engine was out.
The splash of water soaked everybody on one side
so they all went to the other side.

GUS PITTS

TWO YEARS AFTER WWII, A GROUP OF WEALTHY SPORTSMEN LEASED
an abandoned naval torpedo testing station next to the pier in Fort Pond
Bay. They put in a bar, restaurant, tackle shop, and called it Fishshangri–
La. The allure of this makeshift sportfishing marina resulted in even more
crowds piling on the Fisherman's Special. Spaces on the few boats operating
from Fort Pond Bay had always been limited, but with Fishshangri-la
aggressively marketing Montauk, the situation turned dangerous during
the years 1947–51.

Captain Eddie Carroll was the owner and operator of the forty-two-
foot open boat *Pelican* docked at Fishshangri-la. The vessel weighed fourteen tons, one ton below the minimum for mandatory Coast Guard in-
spections. She was powered by two 100-horsepower Chrysler engines.
Captain Carroll's plan that Saturday was to head for Frisbees Shoals, just a
few miles southwest of Montauk Point. He did not plan to fish the next day,
Sunday, because he was getting married.

September 1, 1951 began as a beautiful day. The *Pelican* left the dock on
Fort Pond Bay with sixty-four souls onboard.

Ralph Pitts: *We were over at Watch Hill that morning the* Pelican *turned
over. We got over there and it was just as bright as this. And then all of a
sudden it got dark, you could see the lights on the hanger* [in Fort Pond

Bay]. *I was with Willie and I said, "Willie, we're either staying here tonight or we're going," and he said he wanted to go home. So we dumped over our bucket of chum and took off for home and we had some ride. We had it behind us the whole way.*

Bob Tuma: *I happened to be on another channel and I heard some guys from Rhode Island talking about how bad it was blowing. It was beautiful that day, like a lake before that squall started.*

Frank Tuma remembers, "I came in ahead of the *Pelican* that day. I wanted to beat the tide at the lighthouse."

"I did too," recalls George Potts. "I got in about the same time you did. I saw your father and he said take me out, so we jumped in the boat and ran out there and of course it had already been down."

The *Pelican* started for port at 11:30 AM when the weather turned bad, but there was engine trouble. Only one of the Chryslers was operating. This, combined with an increasing head wind and heavy seas, slowed the *Pelican's* progress. It took two hours for her to reach the lighthouse.

Coming across what locals call North Bar just inside Montauk Point, the *Pelican* ran into heavy seas exaggerated by strong tides. Passengers lined the railings on both sides of the boats, others stayed below in the cabin. When a big wave hit the starboard side soaking the passengers, they ran to the opposite side. Already overcrowded and now unbalanced, the boat capsized when it was hit by a second huge wave.

Gus Pitts was close to the *Pelican* when she went over: *I was fishing at number three [buoy] right by them. He came around the Point and one engine was out. The splash of water soaked everybody on one side so they all went to the other side.*

The boat capsized when the next wave hit it. Gus Pitts saved six people and tried to save the captain: "I threw him a life preserver, but he went down."

Two other boats, the *Betty Ann* with captain Harold Bishop and the *Bingo II* with captain Lester Behan, were able to rescue thirteen passengers from the water, but their capacity was limited and the ocean was extremely rough.

When news of what had happened spread to the harbor, Frank Mundus on the *Cricket II* and Carl Forsberg on the *Viking V* ran out to the *Pelican* and were able to secure tow lines to the hull.

Paul Forsberg recalled the story as his father told it: *They were west of Shagwong when the Coast Guard came along. It was an 83-footer from New London. The wind was out of the northeast and they rolled bad. By the time they came to Montauk they came right into the harbor. The crew was all seasick including the captain. They were all dressed in white and looked so beautiful. They tied up at the dock, and people were all over the dock. They knew boats were out there and they knew the* Pelican *had turned over. Women were screaming at them. "We don't have orders, we have to have orders before we can go out."*

Once the Coast Guard got out to the scene, they demanded the tow lines Forsberg and Mundus had secured.

Paul Forsberg: *Of course they backed right over it and got it in the wheel. They limped in and the boat went down. Fortunately, my father had sent his mate overboard with a line when the* Pelican *popped up again. Just then the Coast Guard 38-footer from Montauk came out and they passed the line to him. All the time the boat had been drifting with the flood tide so they were only a short distance from the jetty. After my father got it tied up he went over to help get the bodies out. When my father came home — we lived in Amagansett — he walked in the house and asked my mother for a cup of coffee. He poured some kind of liquor in the coffee. He sat there and started crying. I never saw the man cry.*

The next day the job of reclaiming the bodies continued.

Gus Pitts: *One guy he was trapped between the two engines in the engine room. We had to chop open the deck with an axe to get him out. One of the troopers went down into the front cabin and he couldn't take it. He came out so I went down and got him out.*

I remember that day standing in the cockpit of my father's first sport-fishing boat. We were docked at the Yacht Club. The weather had turned grey and cold. I was six years old. No one told me what was happening. There were people unloading from boats at the far end of the dock. I saw them coming down the dock all wrapped in blankets. Other people supported them as they staggered over to the clubhouse. Years later I realized that these were the survivors. The dining room had been opened for them while a temporary morgue had been set up at Duryea's Ice House.

Forty-five people, including Captain Carroll, drowned. The disaster scared fishermen and depressed business for some time. "It really killed the business," says Ralph Pitts. "After that, every time you'd get a party, the first thing they wanted when they got on the boat were the life jackets. Quite a bailiwick. Everyone would get aboard and they'd try jigging a rod with a life jacket on."

As a result of the disaster, the Fisherman's Special was cancelled, Fishshangri-la shut down, and the boats that serviced the railroad customers moved over to Montauk Harbor. Fort Pond Bay, its homes and docks pounded by the '38 hurricane, then confiscated by the Navy, cursed by a tragedy, and finally abandoned by thousands of railroad fishermen, could no longer function as Montauk's fishing center. The area began a gradual transition from a central village into the tranquil beach tourists and locals enjoy today.

Two miles east in Lake Montauk a new culture was emerging.

*For the full story of the *Pelican* tragedy readers should look to Tom Clavin's extraordinary book, *Dark Noon*.

Fishshangri-la was big news for Montauk, but only stayed open for five years. © Montauk Library, Al Sari Collection.

THE
GOLDEN
AGE

Perhaps I should not have been a fisherman, he thought.
But that was the thing that I was born for.

ERNEST HEMINGWAY, THE OLD MAN AND THE SEA

The first giant bluefin brought in to Montauk. Caught by Kay Topping fishing with Capt. Don Gross on the *Captain Don*. Far left is N.Y. Yankee owner Dan Topping. ©Montauk Library. Dave Edwardes Collection

BIG FISH

*We wound up with the chair on its side. He pulled the bolts
right out of the wood. Don't forget, at that time we
knew nothing about giant tuna fishing.*

RALPH PITTS

IN THE EARLY YEARS OF THE TWENTIETH CENTURY, BIG GAME FISHING
— swordfish, marlin, giant tuna, sailfish — was a sport limited to an elite
community of fishermen. Ernest Hemingway was fishing out of Bimini in
the Bahamas as early as 1935. The Florida Sailfish Club was founded in
1914 and the International Game Fish Association, the body that would set
the standards governing sportfishing, was established by Michael Lerner
in 1939.

Carl Fisher had successfully used deep-sea fishing to promote Miami
Beach, then he attempted to promote Montauk as the fishing capital of the
world. Fisher considered it the "ideal sport for affluent, out-of-shape busi-
nessmen." Right or wrong, by 1938 there were still very few boats running
out of his Montauk Yacht Club. Frank Tuma brought his first boat to the
Yacht Club in 1940: "There was an abundance of fish in those days. We had
boats that did ten knots and if we traveled an hour and a half at the most,
it was a big day. The war came along and sort of ended things for a while."

East Hampton resident and author Kip Farrington Jr. published his
book *Fishing the Atlantic* in 1937. That volume included a review of the fish-
ing, lodging, and boats available in Montauk. Farrington, the son of a New
Jersey stockbroker, was a respected figure in the sportfishing community.
He was the fishing editor of *Field & Stream* magazine and a friend of Ernest
Hemingway.

His interest in sportfishing began when he moved to East Hampton in the 1920s. His book came out when the Fisherman's Special was still carrying customers to the boats at Fort Pond Bay. Farrington wrote about fishing on the open boats, but also acknowledged that the Yacht Club was home to a small number of private and charter boats whose captains and owners had one overarching goal: to catch a broadbill swordfish.

Swordfish are not as strong or as fast as tuna, nor do they tear across the ocean in a series of dazzling jumps like a marlin. But swordfish, or broadbill as they were commonly called, are notoriously difficult to catch. Nighttime bottom feeders, they are generally not hungry when they come up during the day. Cruising just below the surface, swordfish can be spotted by their two unmistakable sickle fins. Only then will a bait be put in the water and the boat attempt to "present" the bait to the fish by trolling it slowly past the lethargic, seemingly sunbathing, swordfish.

Frank Tuma: *Seeing a swordfish in those days was not a major problem. But once you saw them, getting them to take the bait, or even look at it, and then hooking them, the odds were pretty difficult in each area. I think there were a lot more swordfish hooked than caught. With that bill they were a tough fish to catch. The line would get cut, or there would be a kink in the wire leader.*

While the private boats at the Yacht Club regularly went after swordfish using a rod and reel, charter boats, like commercial boats, preferred to use harpoons. For good reason: swordfish, then as now, was considered a delicacy. A 300-pound swordfish could sell for $90, which was more than twice what charter boats were charging for a day's fishing.

Frank Tuma grew up fishing with his father, and his father was an excellent harpooner: *He really loved it. He could hit those fish. He was left-handed the way he'd throw that pole. I don't care if he saw ten swordfish a day, he would be as excited about the tenth one as he was with the first. One day, when I was about six or seven years old, he had a boat called the Junior. It had a thirty- or forty-foot mast, and he'd tie me up in the yardarm with him looking for swordfish. One day we saw a fish and he was so excited he knocked me right out of the mast. I landed on the pilot house.*

The unmistakable twin sickle fins of a swordfish. ©Akin Collection

Bill Wesner prepares to harpoon a swordfish circa 1962. ©Montauk Library. Dave Edwardes Collection

George Potts (right) at Gosman's Dock circa late 1940's. ©Montauk Library. Margaret Potts Collection

Legendary captain Buddy Merritt kneeling, Fred Solana standing, angler unknown. Circa 1950. ©Montauk Library. Al Sari Collection

In time this preference for the harpoon would change in a big way as captains recognized there was a growing number of rod-and-reel anglers willing to hire them to go after a swordfish. This transition was helped along in the late '50s by awards given by my father at the end of the season to charter captains who had boated a swordfish using rod and reel. In 1958 the charter fleet caught a total of forty-nine rod-and-reel swordfish against a total of thirty-one for the private fleet.

As sought after as swordfish were in the late '40s and early '50s, they did not generate enough excitement in the fishing world to attract more than a few devotees to Montauk. That changed when Kay Topping landed the first giant bluefin tuna brought into Montauk. She caught the fish just a mile or two off the Rhode Island coast at Watch Hill fishing with Capt. Don Gross on his boat, the *Capt. Don*. The location was soon named Rosie's Ledge after the boat (and wife) of Montauk local Harry Alfandre. (Alfandre might have been the first to hook a tuna at Rosie's Ledge, but he did not land it.) A couple of years later in 1951, just a month after the *Pelican* disaster, Hampton Bays captain Buster Raynor on the *Scamp II* fishing out of Montauk caught a 961-pound giant bluefin. That got everyone's attention.

Word that there were big tuna near Montauk had already reached South Florida and Bimini, together the center of Atlantic sportfishing. Anglers including Al and Phylis Whisnant, along with renowned guides Allen and Buddy Merritt, headed north. And it's a good thing they did because locals were not prepared to handle fish as strong as giant bluefins.

Frank Tuma: *It would be hard for anyone today who hadn't fished in that era to realize the fish that were there. We could literally go over there in the first year or two, put your anchor down and throw some butterfish into the water and you had giant fish swimming by like pigs coming into the slops. We didn't know how to catch them. They were an unknown species in their size.*

Carl Darenberg: *When they found giant tuna none of us were equipped for it. I remember my first trip over there [Rosie's Ledge]. I had three 9/0's [reels] and one 12/0, and after the first four fish I hooked, I had no reels left. I had to turn around and come home.*

Even years before anyone landed a giant, there were signs that something big was in the water.

Carl Darenberg: *The thing that amazes me the most is that those guys [other boats] used to go bass fishing over there in the fall. They'd start catching bass, and those guys were stripping 9/0 reels. How can you strip a 9/0 reel on a striped bass? Well, damn, the freakin' tuna fish were grabbing them.*

Once the locals got some exposure to other anglers and captains who had experience catching big tuna, things got better. But not right away.

Carl Darenberg: *Al Whisnant hired me for two weeks. He asked if I had any equipment and when he looked at the crap I had he said, "We'd better use my stuff." We didn't have a [fighting] chair then. All I had were those regular office chairs. He said, "I'll try it, but I think we should get a chair if I'm going to fish for two weeks." We didn't even get that far. The chair just split in half the first strike we had.*

We came back in and I called Al Larson in Rockaway, and I said, "Al, I've got to have a chair." He said, "I have one chair left, it's my display model. I'll meet you in Riverhead." Okay. I drove to Riverhead. It was on a platform and I figured I'd just nail that thing down. Well, we went fishing the next day and the first strike we got the whole works took off. Whisnant went right out of it. He says, "Let's go back and get organized." I learned a lot from that guy.

Frank Tuma: *In the early days when we first found the giant tuna we were using Penn Senator reels — 9/0's, 10/0's or whatever. The giant tuna in those days were tearing them up left and right. The first tuna of that size that we started to catch, you'd go out there and they'd just melt the reels.*

Ralph Pitts: *I had this guy, he was a big strapping guy. We hooked this giant and I said, "The first thing you gotta do is let him know who the boss is." That was the first mistake I made. We wound up with the chair on its side. He pulled the bolts right out of the wood. Don't forget, at that time we knew nothing about giant tuna fishing.*

George Verity, Ralph Pitts, Bob Tuma, Don Gross. Early years charter captains at the Yacht Club. Most white marlin were discarded the following day. Circa 1950. ©Montauk Library. Dave Edwardes Collection

Harpooner strikes swordfish from the bow of Capt. Droebecker's *Skip II*.

Frank Tuma Jr. (left) and Frank Tuma Sr. (second from left) congratulate Louis Ruppel on 658 lb. tuna. Circa early 1950's. ©Montauk Library. Dave Edwardes Collection

Sportfishing, even for the biggest fish, was not just a man's sport. Women had always been part of the picture. Chisie Farrington, Kip's wife, traveled with her husband, and years before Kay Topping caught the first giant bluefin in Montauk, Chisie landed two giants in one day up in Nova Scotia. Phyllis Whisnant competed with her husband, Al, even chartering separate boats on the same day. Carl Darenberg remembers her well: "Phyllis was really good, but she got undressed. She kept pulling her clothes off. She was a pisser, she was!"

Big tuna were so hard to catch for a simple reason — they are different from other fish. As explained by marine biologist Richard Ellis in his 2008 book *Tuna: A Love Story,* "Their hearts, relative to their body size, are three times larger than those of many fish, and their blood has an unusually high concentration of oxygen-carrying hemoglobin." Add to this a body shape built for speed and a muscle structure that maximizes swim velocity: "In contrast to many other fish, the body stays rigid while the tail flicks back and forth, increasing stroke efficiency."

Anyone holding on to a fishing rod when a tuna takes off on his (or her) first run knows this. Even with the drag on a 12/0 reel set at forty-five pounds, the angler is helpless as the line screams off the reel. And tuna don't jump or stay near the surface where a boat can help the angler by chasing the fish. Instead, tuna dive. It's not long into a fight that the line usually points straight down. The only option is an inch-by-inch fight until the fish is close enough to the boat where a mate can get a hand on the wire leader.

Guides in Bimini and its neighbor island, Cat Cay, had been struggling to catch big bluefins since the mid-1930s. The fishing had generated enough excitement that the Cat Cay Tuna Tournament was initiated in 1939. By the time giants were discovered off Montauk, captains such as Buddy and Allen Merritt had had years of experience with these fish. Nevertheless, when they came to Montauk, they were outsiders and not immediately popular with the local crews. But they were catching tuna.

Frank Tuma: *They were remarkable. They caught four or five a day. There was a lot of animosity towards them when they first moved in here, but everyone became friendly. They worked in with the community. They brought a lot of people with them which was good, but the fish brought a lot of people as well. But when the tuna were gone, Buddy and Allen were gone. They couldn't catch a striped bass.*

The Merritts also encouraged anglers and boat owners to come to Montauk. "You had Billy Carpenter come up with the washing machine guy, Bob Maytag, and Russ MacGrotty," Frank Tuma recalls. Maytag would eventually bring his Rybovich, *Bimini Babe,* to the Yacht Club. Russ MacGrotty contracted local captain, Don Gross, to build his boat, the *Tumult,* and hired Buddy Merritt to run it for a couple of seasons.

These experienced anglers worked well with the Merritts and a few other southern crews. But even after a couple of years with big tuna, local boats were not always ready.

Frank Tuma: *Al Whisnant would get a tuna up in ten minutes. If you didn't have a crew that could handle him, you were in trouble. I had an old Canadian, Pete LaBlanc, fishing with me one day. We went over to Charleston [on the Rhode Island coast] one day, threw the hook over, and in a few minutes we had a fish on. And you know Al had that fish up to the boat in ten minutes. I was up on the bridge and Pete had the gaff. I said, "Pete, gaff that fish!" He said, "No way, I'm going down below."*

So why were there so many big tuna so close to the Rhode Island shore? The answer was the same then as it is today: big fish eat little fish. And there were a lot of little fish just off the coast back then.

Gus Pitts recalled a trip he made with his father years before to the same area: *I remember my father and I went to Noank one day [on the Connecticut coast near Stonington and Watch Hill]. They said there were a lot of big sea bass and flounder there. It took us eight hours to get there ... with a little power engine. We made a set that night and dragged for one hour. There was a flounder in every mesh of that net. That's how thick the flounder were and the sea bass. We must have had four or five hundred pounds of sea bass. The bag, the wings, and the cotton on the bag was loaded, we couldn't lift it, it would have tipped the boat over. We had to pick it out by hand. That's how thick they were then.*

As hard as giant bluefins were to catch, there was another problem: no market. "I sold two giants, one weighed 700 pounds," remembers George Potts. "And the other 500 pounds. And I sold them for $27 for the two fish. Now you get that per pound."

Fortunately for the Montauk charter boats, giant tuna and swordfish, were not the only fish anglers were after. There were plenty of smaller fish such as bluefish and striped bass even closer to home, and lots of customers who wanted to catch them.

Ralph Pitt's *Margaret III*, early 50's ©Akin Collection

WORKING MAN BLUES, AND BASS

*At night you'd go through a school of stripers and they'd
light up the water like there were a thousand lights down there.*

GUS PITTS

Frank Tuma: *I think charter fishing started way back when the commercial
boats were here. My dad and his brother Charlie had a commercial dragger
and guys wanted to take a ride. My dad would take them out for the day
while he was dragging, and they'd go fishing right off the boat. That was
probably in the early thirties.*

*It just grew from the demands of the community. The people needed money,
and they saw there was an available market to make some money other
than commercial fishing. It just came along because people said, "Hey, can
I go for a ride?" So then someone probably said, "Well, you can pay for the
gas," and the next thing you know it grew and grew.*

Ralph Pitts: *I started in 1940 with my own little twenty-six-foot Jersey skiff.
I docked at the Town Dock on Star Island. A lot of it's missing now. Then I
got another boat and went to the Yacht Club. We got $35 a day and we fished
bass, sea bass, and bluefish. I had to steer that boat with a tiller, I never went
offshore until I got a bigger boat. The inshore fishing was fabulous.*

These early charter boats had some rough edges.

Ralph Pitts: *When I first chartered I had a board across the cockpit near the stern. Just a board with two gimbals in it. And if you happened to have two heavy guys, you'd go over a wave and the board would spring in the middle, and the first thing you'd hear was BANG! And the two guys would be sitting on the deck.*

Much like today, inshore fishing for blues and striped bass sustained Montauk's charter boat business. Catches of swordfish and giant tuna made headlines, but small fish made money. In the early days the season began in April and ran through November. "We used to throw the boats in the water in April, fish them until June," recalled Bob Tuma. "Take them out and paint them to get ready for the summer. The season finished the first of December."

No one took a break in the winter. Frank Tuma drove a truck for the Town of East Hampton, and Carl Darenberg chauffeured yachts to Florida. Years later Ralph Pitts ran his own boat for eleven seasons out of Cotton Bay in Eleuthera. George Potts and his brother John did carpentry work. As George remembers, "As soon as I put the boat up in dry dock, by the second day my brother and I would already be working. The job was always there."

When the season started back up in the spring, boats were mainly catching cod fish. Then in May it was pollock. Pollock is one fish no one talks about today, but pollock were the key back then to getting a good start on the year.

Ralph Pitts: *Pollock was the mainstay. We used to fish maybe sixty trips in May. May was heavy. The whole state of Pennsylvania would come down with their trailers and you couldn't catch them enough pollock. They'd take ten or twelve boats, a fleet of boats. They were good. They caught and kept anything. Nothing went back.*

Frank Tuma: *You had to wait for the birds to find them. I would anchor or drift in the North Bar and look out at Pollock Rip, and the first time you saw a gull make a dive, it was time to go. When you got there you could step from one boat to the other the length of the rip. We used to feed them turkey sandwiches.*

Why there are no pollock around Montauk today is a mystery. Perhaps warmer water, lack of bait fish, overfishing.

Paul Forsberg has a different theory: *A pollock loves a gill net. They commit suicide. They'll run into a gill net like no other fish I know of. And when they started gill netting them up in the Gulf of Maine, that was the end of the pollock. They caught twenty, thirty thousand pounds of pollock in one gill net. I had one friend who went up there. He was a gill netter and he told me if you put a gill net in the water, a pollock will swim miles to jump in it.*

Bluefish and bass also had ups and downs, but always came back. Bob Tuma says, "After the '38 hurricane there were no bluefish. They came back in '47 or '48, but they didn't come back so strong." According to George Potts, "I caught thirteen bluefish and it made the headlines in the paper. All about three-pounders and the guy who caught bass didn't even get a write-up."

Boats fished striped bass in different ways.

Ralph Pitts: *We had to run in and out of the rocks to catch them. The first charter I took at night, we're goin' around the Point and the two guys say, "Oh, I got something." Thing was we weren't moving. I had the bow of the boat on Weakfish Rock, and those guys had hooked the bottom.*

Frank Tuma: *In those days you had to work to catch a bass. We used to haul our boats out to get the shafts straightened and the wheels balanced to make sure there was no vibration. Everything had to be perfect. We used to say that catching a bass was like shooting a wild turkey. It was a real feat to catch a bass.*

Ralph Pitts: *I never went offshore until I got a bigger boat. The inshore fishing was fabulous. We used to go out all day for $35. That was all at the Lighthouse, Shagwong, and Frisbees. We never fished the Pollock Rip or the Elbow. All of the bass fishing was along the beach, you know, North Bar, Caswell's, Tea House. You never fished outside. The north rips? As far as bass fishing, we never even knew that place existed. We used to fish Shag-*

wong in the fall. You never got much there in the summer, but in the fall you always got fish. Linen line, no wire, just linen line and a Jap feather.

Starting from the earliest charter boat days, Gus Pitts's reputation for catching striped bass was undisputed, but he didn't always run charters. Even before 1950 you could get twenty-five cents per pound for bass, and Gus occasionally took advantage of the market.

Gus: At night you'd go through a school of stripers and they'd light up the water like there were a thousand lights down there. I said to myself, I'm going to make myself a net. I made a net that was four hundred feet long with a big bag on it. I went out there one night and saw this school of fish. I slung the net around that school and I had so many fish in there that it took me all night and day to bring them ashore. I must have had at least four hundred and some hundred-pound boxes. When I got done I burned the net because I was afraid those Bonackers* would get a hold of it and catch up everything.

Trolling was the predominant method for catching striped bass, but Gus was always different: *"I was casting mostly. Casting in the surf, or fishing in the surf with cotton lines. That's all we used. I used to fish by myself all the time. I would fish Gardiner's Island, Slim's Way, Block Island, the Point, all the way down to Gurney's. All casting. Ninety percent of my fishing was casting all the way until I quit. I had forty-two years in the charter business. I started in 1932 and I quit in 1974. There were still plenty of fish.*

Gus was a loner and a risk taker. He prided himself on being the best bass fisherman and had a special talent for getting in close to shore: *I was the only one who knew how to fish the surf. It was a dangerous business, but I knew what I was doing. The breakers either come in threes or fours. Before I would go in, I would study it and go in on the third one and then beat the fourth one. The fourth one would go in just over the lines and it would dig up the bottom, and that's where the fish went to pick up whatever the surf dug up.*

*Long time locals who primarily fish the bays and along the ocean beaches.

Carl Darenberg was the first to use wire lines for blues and bass: *That was in 1949 or '50. We started with fifty feet. It was from the Huntington Drum Wire Company out of Florida. It was like magic. It was rough fishing then. We didn't have pork rinds, we had squid and you had to clean it and shape it, then put it in jars with salt.*

Not everyone thought wire was such a great idea. Gus Pitts recalls, "Carl Darenberg started fishing with wire from down south, and then everybody started using it. It took all the fun out of it."

There are a lot of mates who share Gus's opinion about wire. It produced fish but trolling four 300-foot wire rigs also produced some epic tangles. All it takes is for one line to get crossed with another while the angler is reeling in a fish, and what emerges from the water looks like an Osprey nest. Wire, unlike line, has a memory which causes it to twist, turn, curve, and kink when the drag of the lure is eliminated. Bass fishing at daybreak in November is always cold, and trying to untangle a wire nest with frozen fingers has led more than one mate to reach for his fish pliers and cut the whole mess off.

Whether it was dawn in November, or noon in July, the stretch west of the Montauk Lighthouse in front of Camp Hero was then, and still is, a great place to fish blues and bass. But during World War II Camp Hero was a fully operational military base. Boats could not just troll along the beach. Anyone who wanted to go west from the lighthouse needed permission.

Gus Pitts: *In the war they restricted a lot of places. The fishing was very good, especially the cod fishing. But if you went around the Point you needed to get a permit and put a flag up or they would start shooting.*

Fishermen today have to deal with regulations — but at least they're not getting shot at.

From its infancy in the 1930s and '40s charter boats worked whole-day trips. Thirty-five dollars a day, out in the morning, back in the late afternoon. Then in the '50s when Carl, Frank, and Ralph were docking at the Yacht Club, things changed.

Frank Tuma: *When people used to come to Montauk to fish they'd charter myself, Carl, or Ralph. We'd leave around 4:30 or 5 in the morning and get home around 5 or 6 at night. And I'm talking about inshore fishing. Then I think Carl started the two-trip thing, and it grew from there. After that there wasn't a year where we didn't have sixty trips in October and November.*

By then the price for a full day had risen to $50, then $75, and finally $100 by '59.

Private boats were just that, private. According to Frank Tuma, "You didn't have private boats running charters. If people wanted to go fishing in those days, they either went on a charter boat, or they didn't go at all."

The charter business improved every year especially after the fleet was united in the mid-1950s at the new docks along a stretch from Duryea's Ice House to Forsberg's Viking dock. The line-up included: *Francis Ann* (Doug MaCabe), *Skip II* (Walter Droebecker), *Kuno II* (Frank Moss), *Venture* (Boots Kohlas), *Leatherneck* (Frank Pike), *Jean Two* (Charly Kaiser), *Lillian S* (Dick Shultz*),* *Cricket II* (Frank Mundus), *Early Bird* (Fred Thompson*),* *Sportfisher* (George McTurk), *Squid* (Willie Newbury), *Cigarettes* (Vinnie Grimes), *Ginger* (Harry Clemenz), *Captain Don* (Don Gross), *Margaret III* (Ralph Pitts), *Bluefin* (George Potts), *Marie II* (Gus Pitts), *Dawn* (Bob Tuma), *Captain Sonny* (Sonny Smith), *Viking V* (Paul Forsberg).

With so many boats and customers down at the new docks, other businesses sprang to life. Motels on West Lake Drive were built to serve the fishing crowd. Carl Darenberg opened the Montauk Marine Basin in 1955, and beginning in 1957 Uihlein's rental service offered anyone the opportunity to rent a small boat for the day. Three restaurants opened by 4 AM for breakfast: Salivar's, Viking Grill, and Gosman's. Finally, when the Gosman family expanded their operations from fish packing, lobster sales, and a small breakfast-lunch diner into a waterfront complex, the Montauk Harbor area began attracting tourists as well as fishermen and emerged as Montauk's second economic hub. (Today there are nine dinner restaurants, but none open for breakfast.)

Frank Tuma's father opened a tackle shop in the middle of the charter docks and began helping the captains by putting together split charters. By law charter boats were limited to six passengers, but two or three customers were not always willing to pay the full cost.

Frank Tuma: *By split charters, I mean people coming to the dock and either you had one or you had two and you'd put them together. My dad started that and did a tremendous amount of promotion and advertising to build the actual charter fishing industry. He made money and successes for the guys down there. He kept most of the guys going in those days. When I took over the business after he died, I used to do maybe a thousand split charters a year. They don't do that today. I don't know why, it's just not a thing for the market.*

Every customer who steps aboard a boat wants to feel special, so in addition to being a good fisherman, navigator, and mechanic, every charter captain must also be a host and social director. Making customers feel special results in repeat business. Sometimes it even starts before the customer is a customer.

Gus Pitts: *One day I had a party of two people. We had nine striped bass. They left me two bass on the boat and I was going to smoke them. There were two guys on the dock, and they had their eyes on those two bass. They asked me if I was selling the fish, and said they'd buy them. I said, "I'll tell you what I'll do. I'll clean them for you, go down below and get a bag and pack them up for you, and that's a present from me." They took eighteen charters! If I had charged them five dollars apiece for those fish, they probably would have gone home and I would never have heard from them.*

Gus earned the respect of his customers and every other fisherman. Long after Gus retired, his cousin Ralph's comments reflect how he was admired: *Gus really started that bass fishing. He fished the surf with a boat, and that was tough fishing then. He never did much offshore fishing, but the funny thing was that every time he'd go offshore, he'd get a marlin or swordfish.*

Rescued from the Montauk Recycling Center, this sign had stood by the side of Rt. 27 for decades until sometime around 1980.

THE UMBRELLA RIG

I brought it home with me every night, and I always told my party, "Don't tell them anything or I won't take you out anymore."

GUS PITTS

NO LURE CHANGED THE WAY MONTAUK FISHERMEN WENT AFTER BASS and bluefish more than the umbrella rig. In place of a single trolling lure, it resembles a small school of bait fish underwater. The rig consisted of four or five tube lures connected to a heavy wire spreader similar to a small umbrella. The first day Gus Pitts put his contraption over the side, other boats were struggling to catch one bass. Gus loaded the boat. He recalls that being around 1950.

The idea for the umbrella rig came to him in the middle of the night: *I was off at number three [buoy] one day and nothing was biting. I had three brothers on the boat. All were skin divers. They went down and one of them comes up and says, "The bottom is just loaded with stripers down there." I came home that night and I went to sleep. I woke up and got out of bed and went down in the cellar and thought about rigging up something with a lot of teasers and hooks.*

I kept it on the boat for a week. Dave, my mate, thought it was the craziest thing you could put on a line. So one Saturday I said we should put those things on the line. As soon as I threw that thing out, I had five fish on. I came in with fifty-five stripers that day. The rest of the fleet had three. No matter where I went, I caught fish with that rig.

Gus was always a loner, and in no hurry to share his discovery with others: *I brought it home with me every night, and I always told my party, "Don't tell them anything or I won't take you out anymore." My special lure had everyone on pins and needles. Fish were getting scarce, they weren't biting as good as they used to. I could leave the dock at nine o'clock when the other boats were leaving at four o'clock. I was back in at eleven with all the fish, back out again at twelve. And then back out again at three.*

The attitude around the dock got a little testy after the first year Gus had the umbrella rig. Ralph Pitts was caught in the middle of it. Here he is talking to Carl Darenberg: *Do you remember the time you came over and I was president of The Boatmen's Association. One night you came over to Duryea's where I had my boat and asked me to do something about Dickie Vigilant. You said, "He's going to burn my place down." Gus was running out of your place, and Dickie thought you knew what it was Gus was using. Dickie had gotten bagged and you told me he came over and said that "if you don't tell me what it is, I'll burn your house down." But Gus used to put them in his suitcase and take them home every night.*

Apparently, Gus was enjoying the mystery surrounding the umbrella rig as much as he enjoyed catching so many fish. He wouldn't even take a bribe: *Carl Darenberg and Arthur Klorfein offered me ten thousand dollars just to look at it. I turned them down and told them I was having ten thousand dollars of fun with it every day, why should I take your money?*

No question Gus was a great fisherman and a bit secretive, but he was also a smart businessman: *"I kept that rig for almost two years and when I saw that they were going to get wise to it, I sold it to Garcia.* He was paying me for what the manufacturer made. If they made ten thousand of them, then I got paid for ten thousand right away. I was getting ten cents for every lure. That went on for three years.*

Gus was only slightly less guarded with family. According to his cousin, Ralph Pitts: *One night he calls me up and says, "Ralph, I want to show you what we're using." So he comes over to my house and we sat at my kitchen*

*Garcia Lure Company.

table, and he's got these three lures, three tubes. He says this is what he's using. [Almost, but not exactly.] The next morning we go out, and I say to my mate, "Teddy, let's put them out." We get down to North Bar and it's thick fog. Who do I come across in the fog but Gus. And his mate Dave has a fish on and he goes around the stern with it to get it out of sight on the other side, and he yanks it into the boat. And I say to Teddy, "Hey, something's not right here. There's only two of us here in the fog, and if he told me the truth last night, he won't be doing this.

About a week later a guy from Jersey calls me up. He said he's been out with Gus. He says to me, "We're coming out fishing with you next Tuesday, do you have the new rig?" I said no, I don't have it. He says, 'Well, I was out with Gus and I know what it is. I'll show you." He comes on the boat and asks if I have any heavy wire. The only heavy wire I had was number fifteen, and he says we'll try it. We put it out, and man we had a fish on right away just like that. Then he says, "Don't use it. Gus swore us all to secrecy and said we're not supposed to tell anybody."

While Gus Pitts had the secret sauce, other captains were experimenting with their own rigs. One of them came pretty close to the umbrella rig. Carl Darenberg was mating for George Verity, a veteran captain who had fished the East Coast from Bimini to Montauk: *A guy came over from Connecticut. He had a piece of metal with two bars sticking out. He had a spoon on one side and a feather on the other. I thought, "Holy shit, what a mess this is going to be." He said you put the feather in the water and you throw the spoon in and the spoon goes around the feather. I say it sounds logical.*

George says to me, "What are you doing?" I say I'm putting this thing out for the guy, the spoon goes around the feather. And George says, "Oh for Christ's sake, what are you thinking we're a bunch of f--king idiots, get that thing out of there." Then the guy said, "Okay, take me home." And George says alright we'll take you fishing, and I swear that thing worked like a miracle. Just two bars, that's all, a coat hanger.

Capt. Harry Clemenz with his record blue marlin in 1986. His career spanned more than fifty years.
©Montauk Library. Clemenz Collection

BLUE WATER

You got into a school of those little tuna, there were acres
of them. Acres! As far as you could see all around
they were just shining at you.

BOB TUMA

PICTURES OF GIANT TUNA AND SWORDFISH BROUGHT INTO MONTAUK, along with articles on the sporting pages of newspapers, motivated a new group of fishermen to make the trip out east. While inshore fishing for blues and bass still accounted for something like seventy percent of the charter business, by the mid-1950s July and August trips frequently included all-day offshore runs for white marlin, school tuna, and swordfish. The charter fleet averaged about ten to twelve knots, so distances were limited. Nevertheless, these trips, at least until the '60s, presented a new problem: how to get back.

Take away GPS, LORAN, depth recorders, and radar, and most fisher-men today wouldn't leave the dock. These veterans ran offshore with three navigational aids: a chart, a compass, and a watch. They also used three other less-technical tools: their eyes, ears, and noses. They used their eyes to see color changes in the water, ears to hear the surf on foggy days, and their noses because inshore water smells different than the cleaner blue offshore water. The smell of mussels is unmistakable when you pass inside the lighthouse at low tide.

Frank Tuma recalls, "In those days we mostly had a wristwatch and a compass. If we got caught in the fog, we used a leadline to figure out the depth."

A leadline is simply a rope with a heavy lead on the end and markers every six feet. When Carl Darenberg started fishing: *I didn't have a leadline yet, so a guy brought me one for the next trip. I had it on the boat for a year and didn't know what it did. In those days it was a matter of the clock and time finding your way home. We also listened to how the sea was when we got close.*

Keeping track of time and direction went on all day. Ralph Pitts: *You'd go offshore and you'd go south ten to fifteen miles. Then you go east twenty minutes, turn around and go west twenty minutes. You'd come out of the Butterfish Hole on the west side. When you got ready to go home you figured halfway in between and you were fine as the set* [dominant direction of the water] *was usually to the west. But every once in a while the set would go east, and then, oh brother.* (Coming in too far east of Montauk Point in the fog, the next land is the Rhode Island coast, fifteen miles to the north.)

In the 1950s a few boats had radio direction finders, or pinball machines as some called them. These devices picked up radio code signals from various locations. Both the Montauk lighthouse and Block Island each transmitted a signal. But there were two problems: both signals sounded the same to anyone not adept at Morse Code, and for some reason, you could almost never pick up the Montauk signal. Most captains were not fans.

Ralph Pitts: *Half the time you couldn't get Montauk on it. You get Block Island, but not Montauk. Offshore we'd pick up a signal and then coming in, if we made Ditch Plains we were on a good course.* (Capt. Ricky Etzel of the *Breakaway* still remembers the Montauk signal: dash, dot, dot, dash.)

The first LORANs available to civilians were World War II military Air Force surplus issues. Two feet high, a foot wide, and three feet deep, the APN-4 was heavy, unreliable, and ridiculously complicated to operate. My father was an electronics magician, so he kept two of them on the boat just for fun. Others were not laughing.

Ralph Pitts: *The first LORAN I bought I got from Doug McCabe, and it was about three and a half feet high. It came off an airplane. That thing had about five sequences you had to go through. It took me two years to learn how to run it.*

Clear days things were a little easier, especially when the fish were not far off. Bob Tuma recalls, "I'd say we started putting our baits out at about forty minutes. That wasn't far, about six miles."

The color line, a distinct break where the water suddenly transitions from inshore green to deep blue, was another indicator everyone watched for.

Ralph Pitts: *When you got to the MP buoy about three miles offshore you could see the edge, the color change, about a half mile ahead. If you wanted bonita, you started fishing when you hit the color change. If you went another fifteen minutes off, you'd get into the tuna. Then if you wanted to catch white marlin, you'd go back to the edge.*

Bob Tuma: *When you got into those little tuna there were acres of them. Acres of them! You came into the middle of the school and as far as you could see for miles around they were just shining up at you. You kept trolling you just got more and more.*

Twelve to fifteen miles south-southeast of the point the water drops off to thirty fathoms. It forms a kind of basin with shallower water on the west and east sides. The commercial boats called it the Butterfish Hole, and it was an important area for both commercial and sporfishing.

Frank Tuma: *That was an area that produced an awful lot of fish, and that was as far as we probably ever ran in the 1950s. Twelve to fifteen miles, twenty miles at the most. In those days we'd pick up the fish on the western side and then follow them down east in July and August off Block Island, and then back to the Hole in the fall. That was how it was done in those days.*

By today's standards, the boats were not fast, but there were a few that stood out. Gus Pitts says, "The *Marie II* was quite fast. She did about fourteen knots." The Chrysler Crown at 125-horsepower, and the Chrysler Royal at 150-horsepower, both gas engines, were the most popular power choice. But with the fish so close, the limited power and cruising range was not a problem.

Captains and their charter were not the only people on a boat. Frank Tuma pointed out something that rarely gets the attention it deserves: how important your mate is: *When I think of techniques, I think of mates. Your mate is a tremendous asset. I think of Porky Balcuns when he worked for me. There was a guy who loved to fish, and he knew how to fish. He would try different things. The way he used to catch swordfish is he used to jig the bait so the fish would make a lunge for it. Everyone had their own methods. His worked.*

While most of the fishing was done in the Butterfish Hole, swordfish were frequently found much closer to shore. On his rare trips offshore for swordfish, Gus Pitts would head southwest: *Just inshore at Cartwright, about six and a half miles from the Point. The fish ranged anywhere from two hundred pounds and up. And sharks, there were so many sharks. Makos, hammerheads, blue sharks, there was all kinds of stuff like that.*

Ralph Pitts: "*Eddie Parsons stuck a swordfish right under the lighthouse, so close he couldn't go in and pick the pole up after he threw it. The closest one I ever got was halfway between the Point and the MB buoy.*"

There were a few captains, whether because they were impatient or just wanted to explore, who pushed the boundaries. Frank Tuma: *I don't think anyone went much beyond the Butterfish Hole until Don Gross (on the Captain Don), and Doug McCabe (on the Francis Anne). Don was a ranger, he would really chug on offshore. Also Ollie Olson on the Cigarette. They were the ones that probably extended the distance.*

Each year through the late 1950s and into the '60s the charter fleet was joined by new private boats. And these boats were all faster. My father's boat was built in 1952 at Southbay Boat Works in Patchogue, NY. and averaged fifteen knots. We were the slowest boat at the Yacht Club. The majority of the private fleet were southern-built Rybovichs and Merritts. These boats averaged from eighteen to thirty knots. This speed allowed them to fish areas no charter boat could reach. They were also more focused on swordfish and big tuna, not the school tuna and white marlin that were the backbone of the charter fleet fishing in the Butterfish Hole. It was this reliance on the Butterfish Hole that turned out to be the Achilles heel of the offshore charter business.

1959 awards to charter boat captains for catching a swordfish on rod and reel. (first row) Frank Moss, unknown, Ralph Pitts, Doug McCabe, Walter Droebecker; (second row) Harry Clemenz, Sr., Frank Pike, Carl Darenberg, George McTurk, Paul Forsberg, unknown, Robert Akin, Jr., Howie Carrol, George Potts, unknown, unknown. ©Montauk Library. Richard T. Gilmartin Collection

The annual flag raising ceremony at the Montauk Yacht Club. ©Montauk Library. Dave Edwardes Collection

THE MONTAUK YACHT CLUB

I wish I could put time back to when we were at the Yacht Club and the times we had fishing and the fun and enjoyment we got out of it.

FRANK TUMA, JR.

IN THE 1950S THE MONTAUK YACHT CLUB WAS NOT A PLACE, IT WAS A time. Each year the season began the last Saturday evening in June with a formal Flag Raising Ceremony. Four boat owners, in white slacks and blue blazers standing on the dock's promenade deck, sequentially hoisted their corresponding officer flag: Commodore, Vice Commodore, Rear Commodore, and Fleet Captain. A miniature cannon fired blank twelve-gauge shells as each flag, snapping in the afternoon southwest breeze, reached the white crossbeam on the flag staff below the American flag and Montauk Yacht Club burgee. Following the dockside formalities, families, guests, and any small dogs no longer in shock from the cannon blasts would withdraw to the lawn for a glass of champagne. To me this just seemed to be the way things were done. I was eight years old.

The flag-raising, champagne, and cannon blasts reflected a new post-WWII culture as it emerged from the shadow of Long Island's Gatsby society and Carl Fisher's grand dream. The ambience carried over into other aspects of Yacht Club life. Weekend evenings a piano played in the great room where guests and boat owners gathered around a 270-degree mahogany bar that arched from the great room into the reception lobby where an immaculately polished flagstone floor reflected the afternoon sun. Dinner was served in the adjacent dining room: "Gentlemen: jacket and tie required."

Afternoons the dock swarmed with wives, house guests, an East Hampton Star photographer, an occasional celebrity, all hoping to see whatever trophy fish the boats might have captured. Marilyn Monroe was spotted strolling down the dock to visit New York Yankees owner Dan Topping on his yacht the *Yankee Clipper*. The telecommunications and media tsar (RCA and NBC) David Sarnoff hosted queues of business types on his yacht.

> Frank Tuma recalled one charter in particular: *Henry Fonda used to come and charter my boat for a week. In fact, I fished with him for a week and didn't even know it was him until my wife came in the Club and saw him. That didn't impress me at that point in my life. The only thing that impressed me was how many fish I was going to get and was I going to get paid.*

Boat owners who did not have a house in Montauk or East Hampton booked full-season rentals at one of six bungalows extending off the south end of the club house. Deck chairs lined the canopied boardwalk facing Lake Montauk. Known as Skid Row, the occupants were hard drinkers, and each season generated rumors of an affair or some other scandalous behavior.

The music silenced and martinis drained, the days were for fishing. The Yacht Club sponsored a season-long tournament, the Decathlon, where boats competed to accumulate the most points. Scores were awarded for catches of the biggest fish, including swordfish, tuna, white marlin, mako, bluefish, and striped bass. There were categories for men, women, and juniors, and extra points for light tackle. At the end of the season, the top boat was awarded the Captain's Prize: $100 cash each for the captain and mate. Minimal as this reward might seem, competition was intense.

If point totals were close near the end of the season, and they almost always were, the leading boats often stopped at the Point on the way in from offshore on the final day to snag a bluefish or bass. A three-month contest that saw 400-pound swordfish and 700-pound tuna on the scales was sometimes decided by a seven-pound bluefish.

Montauk Yacht Club circa 1959 ©Montauk Library. Dave Edwardes Collection

Final 1958 Montauk Yacht Club Decathlon competition board. ©Montauk Library. Akin Collection

The 1956 winning Montauk Yacht Club team just back from the US Atlantic Tuna Tournament in Point Judith Rhode Island. Seated: Roy Buchez, Bob Maytag, Johnny Harms. Standing: Lenny Babin, unknown, Shelly Lasnovsky, Jim Sarno, Bob Akin III, Robert Akin, Jr., Swede Swinson, unknown, Harry Clemenz. ©Montauk Library. Clemenz Collection

A young Ralph Pitts on his second boat. Bob Tuma's Dawn in the background. ©Montauk Library. Dave Edwardes Collection

Frank Tuma: *There was a lot of camaraderie back then. Among the anglers there was a great sporting interest. We had our tournaments every year and big parties at the end of the season. And every fish caught in those days was under IGFA regulations. I don't think there was ever any interest other than in people going out and catching a tuna other than the sport of it."*

At the foot of the dock, a ten-foot-high and twenty-foot-long score-board kept everyone up to date on the tournament. Each week the thank-less task of updating the board fell to the Club's piano player. In retrospect, he did a remarkable job. Using two-inch-high and five-foot-long strips of wood previously painted dark blue, he employed a fine brush and white paint to hand-letter the date, angler's name, weight, and line strength used to catch each fish. The three biggest fish in each category went up on the board. This meant that whenever a bigger fish was caught, a new strip was needed while the least-heavy entry was dropped. The final board deter-mined the awards presented at the season-ending Decathlon dinner. Ster-ling silver trophies went to anglers in all three divisions — men, women, juniors — for the biggest fish in each category. There was a separate board showing the boat, angler, captain, and weight of every swordfish caught.

Sport ethics were exceptionally important. Club members considered themselves sportsmen more than fishermen. The competition adhered to sportfishing rules established by the International Game Fish Association. One Club rule that was strictly enforced was the no-harpoon policy. This prohibited any boat that carried a harpoon from participating in the an-nual tournament. A true sportsman, it was thought, would never consider harpooning a swordfish. Regrettably this local rule disqualified most char-ter boats from entering the competition as they continued, at least until the mid-'50s, to rely on harpoons to land swordfish. The economic reward was too strong.

Out on the dock owners and crews, private and charter, shared fish stories as the boats came home. Back in the clubhouse the dining room was reserved for boat owners and their guests. A separate pub-type restaurant, the Crew's Bar, served the captains and mates. (The Yacht Club's physi-cal structure has since undergone two major "renovations," leaving today's building with barely a fragment of its historical character.)

I didn't fit in anywhere, but it was more fun getting a simple dinner at the Crew's Bar. Local Montauk artist Frank Borth, the creator of the comic strip *There Ought To Be a Law,* had painted the walls floor to ceiling with comic fishing murals. I can still recall one scene depicting a familiar fishing boat climbing over a steep wave. Two greenish passengers hang over the side while a smiling mate shouts up to the captain on the bridge, "Hey Cap, they keep calling for O'Rourke!"

Some owners had fished with the charter captains before bringing their own boats to Montauk. As such, they felt a connection with the community. Russ MacGrotty, a Chevrolet dealer in Queens, donated the first ambulance to the Montauk Fire Department one year after the *Pelican* disaster. Herman Isaacs, a meat renderer from Bridgeport, Connecticut, and recent convert to Catholicism, made a substantial contribution to the local parish. My father, Robert Akin, Jr., in an attempt to encourage more sportfishing, awarded a plaque to every charter captain who landed a swordfish on rod and reel.

New private boats, mostly from home ports in South Florida, arrived at the Yacht Club every year while the local charter fleet topped out around 1953. Ralph Pitts was running the Margaret III and recalled that the charter boats that sailed from the Yacht Club were the *Dawn* (Bobby Tuma), *Gannet* (Frank Tuma, Jr.), *Foretenate* (Carl Darenberg), *Captain Don* (Don Gross), *Captain Sonny* (Sonny Smith), and the *Lone Star* (Norman Dicks from Hampton Bays). Many of these boats had moved to the Yacht Club from Fort Pond Bay after the *Pelican* disaster, and Ralph Pitts remembered it as being a good move for his business: "For me the business started to grow when I moved to the Yacht Club."

Another captain Ralph remembered being at the Yacht Club was Tommy Gifford. Gifford, then and now, was recognized as the most influential fishing guide in the history of sportfishing. By the time he reached Montauk, Gifford had fished with many of the best-known anglers and at every famous location from Cabo Blanco Peru in the Pacific to Bimini in the Bahamas, and finally Montauk. Tommy Gifford is credited with the first use of outriggers and the technique of kite fishing. Gifford's standing in the fishing community helped spread Montauk's reputation. By the late 1950s, the word was out.

Murals done by Montauk artist Frank Borth decorated walls in several bars in Montauk. At the wheel, Capt. Harry Clemenz. ©Montauk Library. Clemenz Collection

Frank (far right) and Bob Tuma (second from right) at the Yacht Club circa 1949. ©Montauk Library. Dave Edwardes Collection

63

It wasn't only owners and their crews who talked up Montauk. For most of the 1950's the Yacht Club's manager was Roland (Mickey) Mc-Cann. The Club shut down in October and Mickey moved south to manage the Bimini Big Game Club. He took his Montauk bartender with him to oversee dock operations. Every year a few of the Yacht Club boats made the trip south, reinforcing the Bimini-Montauk connection.

The fishing in Bimini for white and blue marlin, as well as dolphin, was better than what we had in Montauk. But once back at the dock, it wasn't a better place, it was simply a different world. At the marina, boats seemingly floated in space suspended on crystal clear water. In the evening there were no exclusive dining rooms. No Crew's Bar. Everybody in Bimini — boat owners, boat owners' wives, boat owners' girlfriends, crews, local Bimini natives, and this one small boy — shared in the festivities at Hemingway's favorite Bimini drinking establishment, the old English-style Compleat Angler Hotel & Bar. Calypso songs spilled from open windows filling the tropical nights.

Bimini was my first trip outside the United States. And while it was exciting and somewhat exotic, the distinction faded whenever I saw a few familiar boats in the harbor with the Montauk Yacht Club flag flying from their masts.

The Montauk Yacht Club Flag

Carl Darenberg with Broadway star Lisa Kirk. ©Montauk Library. Dave Edwardes Collection

DATE	NAME	BOAT	W T	LINE	CAPTAIN
		1958			
		BROADBILL			
6/29	ROBT. AKIN, JR.	NIKA	367	24	JAMES SARNO
6/29	I. B. CLARK, JR.	GANSETT II	403¼	39	CARL DARENBERG
7/4	GEO. E. SARANT	GEORGETTE	143	24	BUDDY MERRITT
7/9	GEN. WM. RITCHIE	SIKI	328¾	24	HURLEY
7/17	RUSS MacGROTTY	TUMULT II	333	24	JACK PIERPONT
7/21	HELYN PETERS	LAZY BONES III	146	24	FRED SOLANA
7/21	HELYN PETERS	LAZY BONES III	80	24	FRED SOLANA
7/21	PHYLLIS WHISNANT	HELEN H	141	24	WM. HOLZMAN
7/23	ROBT. AKIN III	NIKA	233	24	JAMES SARNO
7/25	W. HARRY PETERS		177	24	FRED SOLANA
7/25	ORA LONGACRE		262	24	WM. HOLZMAN
7/26	HARRY MAXWELL		449	39	WM. HOLZMAN
7/26	E. L. GRUBER		380½	24	WM. HOLZMAN
7/26	J. S. HOWARD	CALYPSO	201	24	OLIE OLSON
7/31	RAY BRUNJES	DORADO II	219½	24	HARRY RAYNOR
8/2	HELYN PETERS	LAZY BONES III	335½	15	FRED SOLANA
8/2	RUSS MacGROTTY	TUMULT II	114	24	JACK PIERPONT
8/2	ORA LONGACRE	HELEN H	257½	24	WM. HOLZMAN
8/4	JOHN ISACS	WALTIUS	353	24	RAY MAYHEW
8/6	H. J. SIMONSON	HUNTER	173	24	GEO. GRATHWOLD
8/6	GERT MacGROTTY	TUMULT II	151¼	9	JACK PIERPONT
8/9	W. HARRY PETERS	LAZY BONES III	161¾	24	FRED SOLANA
8/11	MRS. E. SARANT	GEORGETTE	180	24	BUDDY MERRITT
8/11	MRS. E. SARANT	GEORGETTE	188	24	BUDDY MERRITT
8/11	BILL AKIN	NIKA	227	24	JAMES SARNO
8/11	MAURICE MEYER	POSEIDON II	319	39	GENE WALL
8/12	CLIFF STEIN	CLIFRED III	416	24	SWEDE SWENSON
8/13	ROBT. MAYTAG	BIMINI BABE	303	15	JOHN HARMES
8/21	BILL AKIN	NIKA	185	24	JAMES SARNO
9/3	BILL AKIN	NIKA	246½	24	JAMES SARNO

1958 Montauk Yacht Club swordfish catch. ©Montauk Library. Akin Collection

Opposite page: Hurricane Carol, "The Forgotten Storm", August 31, 1954 caused extreme damage at the Montauk Yacht Club as well as in Point Judith Harbor, R.I. where many Montauk boats were competing in the US Atlantic Tuna Tournament. Winds exceeded 115MPH at the Montauk Lighthouse and gusts reached 135MPH on Block Island. Montauk was cut off from the rest of the island as water crossed the Rt 27 on the Napeague Straight. Waves washed over the dunes where the Montauk IGA is today.

1954 Hurricane Carol (The Forgotten Storm) damage at the Montauk Yacht Club. ©Montauk Library. Dave Edwardes Collection

Johnny Cassulo and wife Dorothea with a trophy for her women's world record swordfish. ©Akin Collection

IT DOESN'T GET ANY BETTER

It was flat calm like a mirror, so anything you saw that interrupted the surface was a swordfish. Never will there be another day like that.

H.E. MacGrotty

A GOOD DAY OF FISHING HINGES ON A GREAT MANY VARIABLES: WIND speed, wind direction, water temperature, tides, sun or clouds. And fish. Fishermen accept the idea that no day can be perfect. But Friday, July 3, and Saturday, July 4, 1959, were just that — perfect.

A light northwest wind, no more than 10 mph, dropped out by late morning. The fleet was fishing just outside Cartwright shoal on the west edge of the Butterfish Hole. As the ocean turned glassy calm, every boat began to see swordfish.

Frank Tuma: *On one particular day, Joe Gomez was my mate, and my dad went with us. It was the 3rd of July, and we didn't see a fish until noon. And from noon until 5PM we saw about fifteen swordfish. We ended up getting like five commercially with a harpoon. They were all in the 250-pound to 350-pound range.*

Paul Forsberg: *It was the 3rd of July, we didn't have a charter. It was just me and my mate Gene McCann. It was a beautiful slick calm day. I had three harpoon rigs on the boat, three keg lines. I saw Olie Olsen on the Ingred and I knew I was in the right area. Olie went off to the south somewhere, and all of a sudden I looked around and swordfish popped up all over the place. They came up and it was like which one do we harpoon first. It was unbelievable. We wound up with five for the day. So I came in with five swordfish and my father came walking down the dock. My whole cockpit was full of fish. I told him, "Dad, I got five fish here." It was amazing, they were all over the place. He said, "How many rigs do you have?" I said three. He said, "I told you you should have five, you would have had ten fish." I said, "I'm the only charter boat with three, most of them only have one." He said, "Don't ever compare yourself to anyone else!"*

The fleet was bunched together and radio chatter that day was almost comical: "Hey Joey, do you see that fish up front of you?" "No, thanks for the heads up, but I'm baiting one off my port beam."

I asked Harry MacGrotty, the youngest son of the Montauk pioneer sportsman Russ MacGrotty, if he remembered those two days in July: *Well, I certainly remember that day as it was epic in swordfishing. I also don't think the morning was anything, but I remember saying, finally, there's one, and simultaneously there was another and another and I couldn't tell you how many fish there were. We caught one but saw probably dozens. It was really mind-blowing for those of us who had spent hours in a tower to see one fish every couple of days. We would be baiting one fish, and instead of setting up for another try we just went on to the next one. It was flat calm like a mirror, so anything you saw that interrupted the surface was a swordfish. Never will there be another day like that.*

But there was. It is not unusual to get a calm day once an early morning northwest wind drops out, but it is extremely unusual for the calm to last through the next day. Nevertheless, that 4th of July was once again flat calm.

And again everyone saw fish. Many were harpooned or caught on rod and reel. Johnny Cassulo, fishing on his boat the *Dorado*, had caught an average-size fish on the 3rd, then let his wife take over the following day. Dorothy Cassulo's 492-pound swordfish, caught July 4, 1959, on 50-pound test line, still stands as the women's world record today. You can look it up.

On our boat, we put the bait to several fish on the 3rd, but no takers. We did manage to catch one about 250 to 300 pounds on the 4th.

Back then you were lucky to see a couple of swordfish on any given day, and, as MacGrotty said, many days you didn't see any. When all the boats had returned late Saturday afternoon, the only ones that hadn't seen swordfish were the boats that had stayed at the dock. If you fished those days, you never forgot it.

Those two days were perfect.

Dorthea Cassulo with her world record swordfish caught on July 4, 1959, one of the two "perfect days". The record still stands. ©Akin Collection

The first Viking in Montauk circa 1953. ©Montauk Library. Dave Edwardes Collection

WRECK WARRIORS

I don't have any money, but I'm putting all these fish in your name.
The fish check is comin' back to you, and that's the deposit.

CARL FORSBERG, ON HOW HE PAID FOR THE VIKING DOCK LAND

WHILE MONTAUK WAS EMERGING AS A PRIME LOCATION FOR INSHORE sport fish such as bluefish and striped bass and bigger offshore trophy fish like tuna, swordfish, and marlin, another competition was heating up all by itself. "Bottom fishing" wasn't sexy to the private "elite" crowd, but at a fraction of the cost of an offshore charter, it appealed to a large number of less-affluent anglers. By the late 1960s, bottom fishing, especially for cod, was a major part of Montauk's fishing scene. The boats were much bigger than the average charter boat and not subjected to the six-passenger limit.

Cod, more than any other fish, have historically caused the most international disputes. Cod wars raged from 1415 right up until 1976 when England and Iceland settled their differences. Montauk's cod wars never involved the U.S. counterpart to the Royal Navy, but the actions of a few seasoned fishermen included deception, electronic warfare, and a few dirty tricks.

The Forsberg Viking fleet is synonymous with Montauk cod fishing. And it is one of Montauk's great success stories. Today's Viking fleet consists of seven vessels running day and evening fishing trips, a sunset cocktail cruise, daily ferries to Block Island, and weekend ferry service to and from Connecticut. The boats operate out of the Viking docks built by the Forsberg family beside a small parcel of land in the Montauk Harbor area. The deposit on the land was paid for with a load of fish.

Before 1951, the family lived in Freeport, but Carl Forsberg ran down east to do some fishing.

Paul Forsberg: *My father was commercial fishing east of Montauk and would unload at Gosman's. Old man Jack Craft was in real estate and was always on his back. "Forsberg, I got good property right here. You shouldn't be in Freeport." So finally my father came in, and he had a good catch of fish. Craft was on his back again, so my father says, "Gimme the damn papers. I don't have any money, but I'm putting all these fish in your name. The fish check is comin' back to you, and that's the deposit." So then he goes back to Freeport and in the dead of the winter all of a sudden the bill comes for the monthly payment. And who gets that but Mom. Let me tell you, Dad was not a happy camper. Mom's famous words were, "Montauk! they don't even have a traffic light."*

The next year Carl Forsberg brought the Viking V to Montauk, and not just for the fishing. Back in Freeport, the schools were already overcrowded.

Paul Forsberg: *We came from Freeport, which was fifty kids to a classroom, and by the time they took roll call we had to move to the next classroom. So that's one of the reasons my father demanded that we move to Montauk.*

Paul's father chose Montauk partly for the school, but also because it was a great place to fish. According to Carl, you could fish right off the lighthouse and catch all the sea bass and porgies you need. But that's not the way it worked out.

Paul Forsberg: *We get to Montauk and the first thing my dad does is take off and goes to Cox's Ledge forty miles away, which no one ever heard of back then. They all thought the world was flat.*

But Paul's father knew something others did not. One day during World War II when he was running the Viking V as a dragger out of Freeport, he saw a fleet of commercial boats fishing at Cox's. They were handlining codfish one after another. Once Paul and his father started fishing out of Montauk, the handliners were still working Cox's.

Paul Forsberg: *They would come out of Point Judith or Block Island with a thirty-foot lobster boat towing a dory. They would put one man in a dory while the others stayed on the lobster boat. They fished two handlines off each boat, one off either side over a four-inch wooden pulley. Their target was a thousand pounds a day from each man.*

It wasn't long before the Viking built a reputation as the best codfish boat in Montauk. The run to Cox's took four and a half hours each way with only two hours of fishing in between. "You just put the boat in a drift, never turned the drift around," says Paul. "You didn't have to, we only fished two hours. Big codfish every time."

Not everybody was happy about how well the Viking was doing. According to Paul, one or two of the other captains got jealous. They started reporting Paul's father to the Coast Guard because the trips sometimes took thirteen hours whereas his license restricted him to twelve. So, like airliners today, Paul's dad took on a second licensed captain to get around the regulation.

Cox's Ledge continued to produce fish until overfishing cut into the stock in the late '60s. But there were still isolated "hot spots" if you could find them: wrecks. Sunken ships attract fish. Small fish use them to hide while bigger fish, such as cod, hang around for dinner.

Locating wrecks is not easy. It involves science, local knowledge, intuition, and luck. Keeping the location of the wreck secret is even harder than finding one.

Paul Forsberg: *I put a LORAN on the boat and I put a scanning sonar on the boat that was made in Germany. We could see out five hundred sixty fathoms underwater. But you had to get talented on how to use it because it also picked up fish and cold spots in the water. The signal would go out Bong … Bong … Bong, and then if you hit a wreck it was Bong-Beep, Bong-Beep. I didn't take any people with me and spent days looking for a wreck. I found the Suffolk wreck between Block Island and Cox's Ledge. She was a freighter that was sunk by a torpedo during the war. She was just loaded with fish. Then the wars started between me, Lester Behan on the* Peconic Queen,

and George Glass on the Helen *because we had the wreck and I was sail-*
ing at 2 AM and charging the outlandish price of twenty dollars a person.
The other boats were only charging ten dollars. Still, we were filling the
boat and leaving as many on the dock. We didn't take reservations in those
days. We'd go out and fish for two hours and have fish all over the place. It
was amazing.

I was fishing three days a week on these special wreck trips, and the other
boats started following me, chasing me. And I had this transmitter crystal in
an old AM radio, and when you pressed the button and whistled, it knocked
out any LORAN for about two miles. So if there wasn't a buoy on the wreck
they couldn't find it, especially if they didn't have a sonar scanner.

We went round and round, and one day my customers started yelling. The
Peconic Queen *had pulled around and was coming out of the sun from*
behind me. So I yelled to the mate, "Cut the anchor line!" I had the engines
running and we're dragging fish, cuttin' lines off, and people are screaming. I
turned and headed right for him. And his mistake was he stopped. We were
staring at each other, you could throw a rock between the boats. And he had
a scanner by that time, but still needed to take a LORAN bearing. As soon
as he went to turn it on I told my mate to whistle into that radio. Lester
stared across at me and I just smiled.

The most famous post-war civilian shipwreck in U.S. waters was the
sinking of the Italian 697-foot ocean liner *Andrea Doria* in 1956. It sank
somewhere off Nantucket following a collision with the Swedish liner
Stockholm. The wreck was noted on nautical charts, but as Paul Forsberg
said, wrecks were never where the charts said.

Paul Forsberg: *I found the* Andrea Doria *in 1968, and it wasn't anywhere*
near where it was supposed to be. I haven't found one wreck that is where the
charts say it should be. The Andrea Doria *was off by four and a half miles.*
It was fifty-one miles off Nantucket shoals, and that was another commo-
tion because my captain's license was only for fifty miles. Some competition,
I won't mention any names, called me in on the Coast Guard.

The fishing was phenomenal, unbelievable. The pollock on top of the wreck were so thick you couldn't get a bait down to the cod. So we wound up putting a sinker and the bottom hook with a big bait on it in a paper bag wrapped around the line, and dropping it down. When you got to the bottom you pulled on the bag so it would come apart, and the clam would come out and the codfish could get at it.

Today's Viking fleet is run by the third and fourth generation of Forsbergs. Dad wisely stays clear. "I try not to go down there," Paul says, "'cause I see things, and if I say anything, I get in trouble."

Early Frank Mundus (second from right) Monster Fishing. ©Montauk Library. Dave Edwardes Collection

MUNDUS

Frank capitalized on it. He did a good job.
Frank did a very good job.

FRANK TUMA

ALTHOUGH CAPTAIN FRANK MUNDUS, THE ORIGINAL MONSTER MAN, had already retired to Hawaii when we sat down for the Tipperary interviews, what he contributed to Montauk sportfishing must be acknowledged. Frank built the strongest charter franchise Montauk has ever seen, and he did it catching fish no one else wanted: sharks.

Curiously, sharks were not what brought Frank from New Jersey to Montauk. Captain Mundus was fishing out of Brielle when the owner of Montauk's Fishshangri-la came aboard in July 1951 to encourage Frank to bring the Cricket II to Montauk. The Fisherman's Special train was filled to capacity every weekend, and there were not enough boats to handle the crowds. So Frank made the move with his wife and young daughter, Bobbie. They didn't have a place to stay, so the Cricket II was both family business and family home for the first season.

In New Jersey, most bluefishing was done by spooning overboard ground-up fish meal, usually bunkers, to attract the fish. But when Frank tried this method off Montauk, he discovered that instead of bluefish in the slick, he attracted sharks. Even more to his surprise, Captain Mundus discovered that his charter customers were far more excited to go Monster Fishing, as he called it, than spend the money on just another bluefish trip.

Nevertheless, bluefish and bass were still the mainstay of Montauk's charter business with offshore trips for swordfish, marlin, and school tuna as a July-August bonus. In the 1950s and '60s, with the exception of makos, sharks were not considered true sport fish by traditional anglers for three reasons: they were too easy to catch, they didn't fight as hard as the other game fish, and there were too many of them.

> Frank Tuma: *In the '50s, if people wanted to fish for sharks, we laughed at them. Makos were the only shark that counted. On a normal day offshore you always saw sharks, mostly blue sharks, and sometimes dozens. If one came up behind a trolling bait, we would speed up and pull it away from him.*

But Frank Mundus didn't care what others were thinking. He saw that thousands of people outside the small clique of sportfishermen were fascinated with sharks. Frank Tuma typifies how Mundus was respected by his fellow fishermen: "Frank capitalized on it. He did a good job. Frank did a very good job."

Mundus built a reputation and a loyal following on the fish that others ignored. And he did it all before the Benchley-*Jaws*-Spielberg media feeding frenzy. After that, Frank Mundus, the Monster Man, became the best-known celebrity who could honestly call Montauk home.

After retiring, Frank Mundus became a critic of the old fishing mentality. He was a strong advocate for catch and release fishing as well as the use of circle hooks. He knew what had happened to the fishing, and it hurt him.

In July 2007, Frank returned to Montauk from his home in Hawaii for his last visit. I stood in line at the Star Island Marina one afternoon with his book *Fifty Years a Hooker*. I wanted his autograph in my copy. When it was my turn, I introduced myself by saying that I was just a boy when he was most active in Montauk. Then I mentioned the *Nika*, my dad's boat. Frank looked up at me, and I remember his few words: "Oh, you know what it was, you saw it."

THE
DEEP SEA CLUB

*A sportfishing boat is like a stallion waiting for someone to open
the stable door. "Go ahead," it says, "throw off these lines.
I want to run." And that's what they did.*

BILL AKIN

THE MONTAUK YACHT CLUB WAS MANAGED BY THE MONTAUK BEACH
Company, Inc., an entity created to sell off the assets of Carl Fisher's
bankrupt Montauk Beach and Development Corporation. Operating a
growing sportsman's marina was not a priority for the Beach Company.

By the end of the 1950s there were serious problems at the Yacht Club.
Summer mornings a fleet of at least fifteen boats left the dock most days.
When they returned, every boat needed to refuel, take on ice, and wash
down. Fish, anywhere from small bluefish to giant tuna, were gutted and
cleaned right on the dock.

The employees hired by the Beach Company to run the dock were
not up to the service required by the fleet. The Dock Master, Rex, always
dressed in a khaki uniform and wore a Navy cap. Rail thin, black mustache,
and never without his pipe, he resembled the Alec Guinness British Colo-
nel prisoner of war character in *Bridge On the River Kwai*. His eccentricities
would have been acceptable if Rex didn't clearly dislike sportfishermen.
His ideal customer stayed tied to the dock. Rex's July/August "staff," two
well-meaning but inadequately trained college kids, were not much help.

Boat owners had seen what better service was like at other marinas up

Harry Clemenz (left) with renowned guide Buddy Merritt. ©Montauk Library. Clemenz Collection

and down the coast. Then in 1958, Mickey McCann was fired as the club-house manager and the boat owners' patience ran out.

Part of the solution, in the form of Carl Fisher's abandoned Star Island Club gambling casino, lay three hundred yards north of the Yacht Club. The other piece of the puzzle lived in East Hampton in the person of John Olin, Chairman of the Board of the arms manufacturer Olin Mathieson Chemical Corporation. Olin was friendly with a couple of the most disgruntled Yacht Club boat owners. Working together, the money was raised to buy the old casino and the small adjacent dock. In 1959, the Montauk Deep Sea Club was born.

The casino was renovated to include new dining and bar areas along with a casual restaurant in the basement that served daily breakfasts, lunches, and dinners to all customers. Social class distinctions had begun to evaporate, so the new restaurant adopted the all-inclusive Cruise Bar designation in place of the Yacht Club's Crews' Bar. The owner of the Amagansett restaurant, Spring Close, was hired to run the main dining room.

The new owners also hired Carl Darenberg's brother, Bobby, to run the dock. At last fishermen had someone who knew what they needed in charge of the operation.

The dock was rebuilt with all new pilings and a weigh-in station. A six-foot-wide white canvas runner stretched the length of the dock.

Throughout the 1950s the charter boats had gradually left the Yacht Club and moved over to new docks by Duryea's Ice House, Tuma's tackle shop, and Salivar's Restaurant. Then in 1960 the entire fleet of private boats relocated to the Deep Sea Club. With this move, the soul of the Montauk Yacht Club slipped away. The club lived on in name only.

With an expanded charter fleet lined up at the Duryea/Tuma/Salivar docks and a collection of the newest, fastest, and best equipped private boats anywhere on the coast at the Deep Sea Club, Montauk was primed for a new chapter.

There was energy everywhere. Even the boats — Rybovich, Merritt, Hatteras, Prowler — seemed restless. Walking down the dock at night you could feel their energy. Unlike parked cars, boats can't hold still. Tides flow beneath their keels and ripples lap their water lines sending reflections up their sleek hulls. And always the smell of life from the water. A sportfishing boat is like a stallion waiting for someone to open the stable door. "Go ahead," it says, "throw off these lines. I want to run." And that's what they did.

The Deep Sea Club attracted new owners that shook up the old guard.

One boat was not enough for Johnny Cassullo. The *Dorado* was a forty-foot Andy Mortensen and the *Ahi* a much faster thirty-two-foot Prowler for calm days. Each boat with its own crew. Johnny's business was based in Brooklyn and had something to do with essential oils. No one really knew much about it, not even his captain. Johnny flew in on Fridays by seaplane along with his stunning wife, Dorothy. The plane landed in Lake Montauk and taxied up to the Deep Sea Club dock. One winter when all was quiet in Montauk, Johnny chartered a friend's boat in Panama. He flew down with his captain and mate. At night, somewhere between Panama and Columbia, the boat disappeared. No trace of the boat, Johnny, Captain Clarence Fine, or the mate, Chuck Fine, was ever found.

Bob Maytag wasn't a newcomer, but he was an electrifying character. Heir to the Maytag Appliance and Maytag blue cheese fortune, Bob brought two boats to Montauk: the *Bimini Babe*, a forty-foot Rybovich, and the *Baby Babe*, a smaller, faster version. Walking past the *Bimini Babe* on the dock in the evening people were caught off guard by the bikini-clad model sitting cross legged in the tuna tower sipping a martini. It was a mannequin, but at first glance, and everybody glanced, she looked very real.

More than anything, Maytag was a fishing fanatic. When he heard stories about huge perch in Africa, he shipped one of his boats to Lake Rudolf, an alkaline lake bordering Kenya and Ethiopia. He took his crew with him to this place no one had ever heard of, fished the lake, caught several 200-pound perch, and filmed it. I saw the movie.

Bob Maytag was a fun guy and an unapologetic playboy. He was also a heavy drinker and passed away at age 38.

Dinny Phipps, whose great-grandfather was Andrew Carnegie's partner, only had one sportfishing boat, the *Fighting Lady*, but he also had a yacht. The *Vergimer*, about ninety feet and referred to as "The Lunch Wagon," followed the *Fighting Lady* to whatever port Dinny was fishing from. He was a stout man and enjoyed a good meal after a day on the water.

A big mako attacked this swordfish on the surface before mates Jim Donovan and Chuck Fine salvaged the remains. Jim is now a member of the IGFA Hall of Fame, Chuck Fine disappeared in between Panama and Columbia along with boat owner Johnny Cassulo, and Capt. Clarence Fine. ©Montauk Library. Akin Collection

A day's catch at the International Fishing Championship. Kneeling: Jack Stevens, Billy Holtzman, Bob Linden, Standing: Commodore Dato Thompson, Ed Gruber. ©Montauk Library. Akin Collection

Dinny's visits to Montauk only lasted a couple of years, but he remained a respected supporter of the sportfishing community for decades.

With only one boat, and a small one at that, Jack Rounick could not compare with Maytag, Cassullo, or Phipps, but he made up for it in other ways. Unlike the other owners at the Deep Sea Club, Jack was a newcomer to the sport. His business was socks, and he liked to party. His initial boat, the *Alligator*, was one of the first fiberglass Hatteras hulls. Cruising speed was barely sixteen knots. He kept the boat for two years before deciding it was way too slow.

Jack's next boat, again the *Alligator*, was a thirty-seven-foot Merritt powered by two supercharged Chevy 409 engines. The boat didn't float, it flew. In the 1960s, forty-two knots was just stupid fast. When other private boats were trolling east of Block Island, or cruising the Dumping Grounds off Martha's Vineyard, the *Alligator* with Capt. Jimmy Donovan was stalking swordfish east of Nantucket. Out and back the same day.

George Sarant's boat, the *Georgetta* (wife's name Etta) was long and slow. Frustrated by the lack of powerful marine engines, gas or diesel, Sarant went back to his business in Freeport to think things over. He was a Ford dealer and knew a lot about engines. A year later he repowered the *Georgetta* with two 534-cubic-inch V-8 Ford truck engines converted for marine use. It worked. Rebranded as Seamasters, the high-torque, low-RPM motors were dependable and powerful. Seamasters sold well for years.

Montauk's own Harry Clemenz grew up working on his father's charter boat, the *Ginger*. By the '60s he was running a nondescript private boat, the *Doc's In*, out of the new Sea and Sky Portell on East Lake Drive. Harry mostly ran the boat for the owner alone, no mate. But Harry was catching swordfish, a lot of swordfish — more swordfish than anyone else with the possible exception of Billy Holzman on the *Nitso*. As a courtesy, the Deep Sea Club let Harry weigh his fish in at the club's scale as the Portell had no weigh-in station. They'd never admit it, but watching Harry bringing in fish week after week got to be a little frustrating for some of the other owners with super-fast boats and two — or even three-man crews. Harry was a good fisherman, plain and simple. And he proved it in Montauk for the next forty years, most notably when in July 1986, again working without a mate, he caught the biggest blue marlin ever brought into Montauk, 1176 pounds.

The Deep Sea Club boats, together with a reenergized charter fleet, were catching fish and gaining attention from Long Island and New York newspapers, fishing publications, and fishermen worldwide. The result was an event never before or since attempted: The 1965 *Peoples to Peoples International Fishing Championship.*

Inspired by Dwight Eisenhower's 1956 Peoples to Peoples program, and organized by Commodore John Olin and Vice Commodore Dato Thompson, a Cadillac dealer from Cincinnati, the event drew two-man teams from the US.. Virgin Islands, Bermuda, Spain, Argentina, South Africa, Australia, and New Zealand. The U.S. was represented by four teams: Atlantic Coast, Pacific Coast, the Deep Sea Club, and a women's team.

Al Wisner, writing in Motor Boating magazine, explained: *The purpose of the International Peoples to Peoples Fishing Championship is not so much to name a fishing champion as to give an opportunity to a group of international sportsmen to get together to help foster the objective of peaceful relationships between nations through understanding and mutual respect of individuals.*

A dinner-dance reception was held at Gurney's Inn, the awards ceremony at the Deep Sea Club, and a farewell breakfast once again at Gurney's. The winning team was the host team, second place the U.S. women's team, and third place, the New Zealanders. The two day catch totalled thirteen swordfish. Looking back fifty-four years, I consider that tournament the pinnacle of Montauk sportfishing.*

But currents were changing even as the *Peoples to Peoples Championship* successfully concluded. Expanding use of commercial longlines had already begun to impact swordfish stocks, new boat owners were less likely to join the annual competition, and technology was beginning to influence where and how boats fished.

Billy Holzman, a Hampton Bays local, ran Ed Gruber's forty-four-foot

SCHEDULE OF EVENTS
(Tentative)

SATURDAY, JUNE 26, 1965
Pre-Tournament Meeting — Deep Sea Club
Cocktails and Dinner

SUNDAY, JUNE 27
Fishing All Day
Cocktail Party — Deep Sea Cl
Dinner and Entertainment — Gurney's

MONDAY, JUNE 28
Fishing All Day
Cocktail Party — Place to be announc
Dinner and Dancing — Gurney's

TUESDAY, JUNE 29
Fishing All Day
Cocktails and Lobster Cook Out — Gurney's

WEDNESDAY, JUNE 30
Fishing All Day
Cocktails and Dinner — Gurney's
Monte Carlo Party

THURSDAY, JULY 1
Final Day of Fishing
Awards Dinner and Trophy Presentation — Deep Sea Cl

FRIDAY, JULY 2
Day of Departure
Champagne Breakfast — Gurney's

A special program of on shore activities
for visiting ladies to be announced.

INTERNATIONAL FISHING CHAMPIONSHIPS

JUNE 26 thru JULY 1
1965

MONTAUK   NEW YORK   U.S.A.

Brochure cover for International Fishing Championship. ©Montauk Library. Akin Collection

AWARDS

The tournament committee is pleased to announce that the winning team will receive one new 1965 Cadillac automobile — complete with full factory equipment, including air conditioning.

FOR THE TOP BOAT

The committee guarantees to the boat producing the high overall point score the sum of

$5,000

In Addition

Many other valuable prizes are assured for the top anglers and other substantial cash prizes, to be determined by the number of entries, will be posted for the top boats and crewmen.

Awards

Accomodations

General Information

Itinerary for 1965 International Fishing Championship. ©Montauk Library. Akin Collection

Rybovich, *Nitso*. Swordfish were the only fish Gruber cared about. Everyone knew the swordfish moved east as the season progressed, but Billy connected the movement to water temperature. Within a year of the '65 tournament, the *Nitso* left Montauk in mid-July for Nantucket, and colder water. Other boats followed for the last weeks of the summer season. But to those, like my father, who stayed on in Montauk, it was clear the old gang was breaking up.

Friday afternoon at the Deep Sea Club. RM Akin Jr. on ladder. Johnny Cassulo flies in for the weekend. Notice the white canvas dock runner. ©Montauk Library. Dave Edwardes Collection

*A personal opinion: In the 1970s and '80s there was still some good giant tuna fishing, especially 1977 when several fish over 900 pounds were caught, the biggest weighing 1071 pounds. Swordfishing, however, continued to decline.

The mostly new and faster boats at the Deep Sea Club 1960. ©Montauk Library. Dave Edwardes Collection

WHAT
HAPPENED

*There is no folly of the beasts of the earth
that is not infinitely outdone by the madness of men.*

HERMAN MELVILLE, *MOBY DICK*

As many as ten foreign factory ships (trawlers) operated in the waters just outside the 12 mile international fishing boundary before it was extended to 200 miles in 1982.

CAT FOOD AND RUSSIANS

Oh yes, the fishing was good until they started trash fishing ...
that's when they cleaned the place right out.
They took everything. They just killed it.

RALPH PITTS

BIG FISH EAT LITTLE FISH IS THE FIRST LAW OF THE OCEAN. WHERE there are little fish, there will be big fish. It's predator and prey. In the Montauk area swordfish feed on a variety of small bottom fish such as butterfish, whiting, ling, and small cod. Swordfish have huge eyes and cruise near the bottom at night. They are not picky eaters. Cut open a swordfish stomach on the dock, and you'll find all sorts of creatures, maybe even a crab or a small lobster.

Tuna tend to stay closer to the surface feeding on herring, bunkers, mackerel, or squid. But they'll make an occasional pass along the bottom. The big-eat-little law holds for inshore fish like bluefish and bass as well.

From the earliest days of the twentieth century, the Smith Meal Company, the same company that had hired Gus and Ralph Pitts' fathers, had a manufacturing plant six miles west of Montauk at Napeague, or Promised Land as it was locally known. The business depended on menhaden, aka bunkers, an oily fish used for fish meal and dietary products. Decades of overfishing up and down the Atlantic coast by their fleet of seiners caused stocks of menhaden to collapse by the middle of the twentieth century. In a desperate effort to save the company, Smith Meal put word out to local commercial fishermen that the company would buy any fish of any size. If there was no other market, they would sell it as cat food. Montauk sport-fishing would never recover from this decision.

The Butterfish Hole, twelve miles south-southeast of Montauk Point, was the go-to place for offshore fishing in the 1950s. It was accessible to both private and charter boats, most of which had a cruising speed of no more than ten to twelve knots. In July and August the fishing was excellent.

Local bottom trawlers using traditional gear had fished the area for decades, coexisting with the sport fleet. But when Smith Meal announced they would buy any fish, a few local trawlers began using nets with extremely fine mesh. It became known as trash fishing, and that changed everything.

The fishermen we interviewed were unanimous in their condemnation.

Frank Tuma: *They meshed their nets so that they could get anything. They sank about two boats. They would come in with a sixty-five-foot boat with a freeboard of eight inches. They'd come in with their bags hanging, and in two years they cleaned it out.*

Gus Pitts: *Dick Stern. He sank one boat. He put so much fish on it that he sank the boat. The mesh was so small you couldn't shove your little finger in the mesh.*

Ralph Pitts: *Oh yes, the fishing was good until they started trash fishing … that's when they cleaned the place right out. They took everything. They just killed it. There were three or four boats over the course of a few years that got overloaded and sank. They used to come in with just the deck above water they loaded them so heavy. That lasted about three or four years and then they cleaned it out. That's the reason you don't have any fish today… If you take the bait away, the fish aren't going to come here. You just can't do it.*

Frank Tuma: *Now I'm not anti-commercial fishing, but they literally went out and emptied out the Butterfish Hole as far as bait fish. From that time on, our whole fishing changed in the area.*

Gus Pitts: *When they started digging out the Butterfish Hole that's what stopped everything. It took four years for them to dig it out, but they dug it out and sent all that stuff out for cat food. I think they were getting five dollars a ton for that stuff. They were catching everything, small fluke, small flounders, little blowfish, whiting, butterfish, little skates, blowfish, everything and anything.*

Finally, Smith Meal went broke in 1969, and that put an end to trash fishing. But the news only got worse. Montauk fishermen, both commercial and sport, have always shared the ocean with boats from Connecticut, Rhode Island, and Massachusetts. Then in the late 1960s there were some new arrivals.

Until the boundary was changed in 1982, international waters extended to within twelve miles of the U.S. coast. No regulations, come and get it. And they did — Russian, Spanish, Portuguese, and a few others. Known as distant water fleets, these three-hundred-foot super trawlers were capable of catching, processing, and freezing whatever they hauled in all while staying in place for weeks.

As many as ten of these factory ships scoured the bottom off Montauk to Martha's Vineyard starting in the late '60s. On clear days Montauk fishermen heading past the lighthouse were greeted on the horizon by the sight of what looked like a naval blockade.

Paul Forsberg: *Once the foreign fleets were here, they hit everything. They just decimated everything. When they took the ling, the whiting, the yellowtail, what we called trash fish, there wasn't any food here for the fish anymore. The swordfish didn't come in. Why would the tuna come in? Why would the sharks come in? When we were swordfishing, you'd see thirty, forty sharks a day. Blue sharks mostly. You saw turtles, you saw sharks, whales, all kinds of bait. So when that happened, it changed the whole food chain.*

Everyone knew it was a problem, yet some sportfishermen took advantage of these boats. Trawlers hauling back huge nets left a trail of dead by-catch floating behind. The result was a massive chum line and it attracted big bluefin tuna, or giants. Local sport boats backed in behind the trawlers. Tuna would come up slashing the surface inhaling floating by-catch. Throw a bait over and you were almost guaranteed a hook up. It was like shooting fish in a barrel without the barrel.

With the Butterfish Hole depleted and a broader area scorched by foreign trawlers, Montauk captains had to adapt. There were two options — some ran farther offshore while others started fishing down east off Block Island. But without the power and speed of the new private boats, the range of the charter fleet was limited. A third option was sitting, or docking, right under their noses: Frank Mundus.

Frank's *Cricket II* was doing just fine all alone catching sharks. Then when *Jaws* hit theaters in 1975, the whole notion of shark fishing got a huge boost. It took a few years, but shark fishing, something Frank Tuma remembered people laughing at when he started at the Yacht Club, finally emerged as Montauk's primary offshore fishery. By 2000 there were three annual Montauk shark tournaments. Tuna and swordfish tournaments: zero.

LONGLINES AND BIG NETS

You can't kill the pups.

FRANK TUMA

BOTTOM TRAWLING, FIRST BY LOCAL TRASH FISHERMEN AND THEN BY foreign factory ships, damaged the local sea bottom ecosystem. But the mid and surface level waters where most pelagic fish subsist had not yet been exploited by commercial interests. Things changed in the late 1960s.

Americans started eating more fish, both traditionally prepared and as sushi. This resulted in a stronger market, higher prices for fish, and an increase in commercial fishing. Two methods, pelagic longlines and drift nets, became more common. Following migration patterns, these boats operated from a number of ports and ranged up and down the East Coast, generally fishing far offshore.

To Montauk sportfishermen longlines and drift nets seemed to come out of nowhere. Longlines can reach up to thirty-five miles with as many as 12,000 baited branch lines, or snoods. The method originated in Japan and was used as early as the 1940s by tuna fishermen working Stillwagen Bank off the New England coast. Cuban fishermen had also used longlines for decades. And while it is an effective fishing method, back then longlining was a notoriously indiscriminate way to catch fish.

Same for drift nets. Like an underwater fence, drift nets hang at various depths below the surface. Before they were regulated in 1989, there was no limit on their length.

Both methods had a dramatic impact on all pelagic fish especially sword-fish, marlin, tuna, and sharks. By-catch was unavoidable. A boat targeting swordfish would frequently end up with a number of sharks that would then be thrown overboard dead. Or perhaps worse, released after their fins had been cut off. Turtles and seabirds were also casualties of longlines.

Ralph Pitts and his father had both worked as commercial fishermen, but after seeing what longlines had done to the fishery, Ralph's patience ran out: *The trouble today is these goddamn commercial fishermen are not thinking about tomorrow, they're only worrying about today. That seems to be the way with everything, not only fishing. Nobody worries about what's going to happen ten years from today, they're just worried about what they're going to make this year.*

From the early '80s through the '90s no attempt had been made to limit the catch of juvenile swordfish on longlines. Swordfish reach breeding maturity when they are approximately 135 pounds. Catches of fish as small as thirty-five pounds were often brought in to local markets and restaurants.

Frank Tuma: *I've seen in my fish market when I had that seven or eight years ago, this one guy came in with a load of fish. The pile you could have put on this table. The fish were so small. You can't kill the pups. Even harpooning is commercial, but at least with harpooning there's no way you can catch those fish out.*

Ralph Pitts: *You can't keep catching these pups and killing them and think you can still get swordfish. You watch these guys with these longlines when they have swordfish. They have twenty-five or thirty of these pups and they're only eighteen or twenty pounds. They're going to kill it sooner or later. Now they're putting a limit on them, but it's kind of late.*

The limits Ralph referred to were initiated in the late 1980s for drift nets and '90s for longlines. The longline regulations established exclusion zones in three known swordfish breeding grounds: the Gulf of Mexico, Florida Straits, and in an area far off the South Carolina coast. Longline crews were forced to make adjustments to their gear to reduce the catch of juvenile fish. Circle hooks were also eventually required making it easier to release undersize fish. These changes helped to partially restore swordfish stocks and were also beneficial to western Atlantic bluefin that breed in the Gulf of Mexico.

But by the mid-1980s, years of local trash fishing, followed by foreign factory ships, longlines, and drift nets, the fish were in trouble.

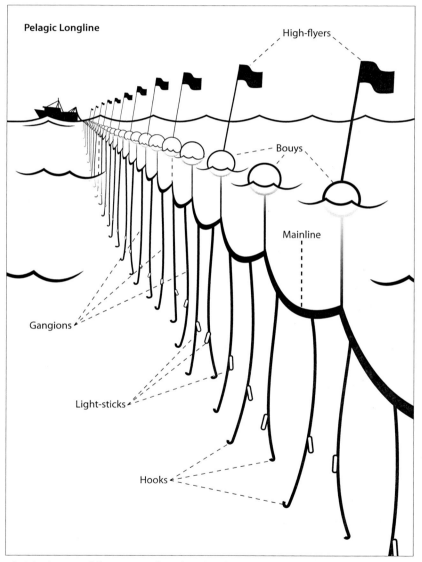

Pelagic Longline

High-flyers

Bouys

Mainline

Gangions

Light-sticks

Hooks

Pelagic longlines extend for an average of 28 miles and can have as many as 10,000 hooks.

REGULATIONS OR STRANGULATION

Then the American Government turned around and made it very easy to get nice big beautiful commercial boats built. A lot of doctors, dentists, and lawyers got into the commercial fishing business.

PAUL FORSBERG

EVEN AS EARLY AS THE LATE 1960S IT WAS CLEAR THE SITUATION WAS getting out of hand. Stocks of both tuna and swordfish were declining. Ten years later with the cumulative impact of trash fishing, foreign factory ships, longlines, and drift nets, the fishing world was a mess.

Even before GPS, better technology — LORAN, depth recorders, radios, radar — enhanced the efficiency of expanding sport and commercial fleets. LORAN, short for long range navigation, took a lot of the guesswork out of where boats fished. Boats could "run to the numbers," meaning precise chart locations. Depth recorders didn't just tell the depth, they showed schools of fish or even an individual big fish passing under a boat at anchor. Radar almost, but not quite, turned fog into sunshine. And radios were like twentieth-century cell phones: some captains hardly ever used them, others couldn't stop talking.

Given the double whammy of technology and fishing pressure, some sort of regulation was inevitable. The United States responded in 1976 by passing the Magnuson–Stevens Fishery Conservation and Management Act, commonly referred to as the Magnuson–Stevens Act. The stated purpose was "to promote optimal exploitation of U.S. coastal fisheries." To say that the Magnuson Act was, and still is, controversial is an understatement of oceanic proportions. The arguments are way too varied, complicated, and emotional to be dealt with here. But some action was needed. Everyone knew that stocks of fish were in decline. Has it helped? "Maybe," "probably," "who knows," and "no way" are all reactions an outsider might hear today. Other responses are unprintable.

Restrictions included the number of fish, the size of fish (not too big, not too small), and even the number of days when fishing was allowed. And the regulations were constantly changing. Both commercial and recreational fishermen were understandably confused and frustrated.

In addition to the Magnuson-Stevens Act, an amendment to the United Nations Convention on the Law of the Sea in 1982 established a 200-mile Exclusive Economic Zone barring foreign commercial boats. At about the same time, the US Government made extremely low interest loans available to domestic commercial fishermen.

The 200-mile limit took care of the factory ships, but the loan provisions resulted in an explosion of the U.S. commercial fleet. It didn't take long for some people to point out that overfishing by foreign vessels had been merely replaced by local boats.

Paul Forsberg: *Then the American Government turned around and made it very easy to get nice big beautiful commercial boats built. A lot of doctors, dentists, and lawyers got into the commercial fishing business. There was plenty of room because we got rid of the foreign trawlers, and they overbuilt the fleet. And they killed everything.*

The Magnuson-Stevens Act also designated the National Marine Fisheries Service as the governing agency "for the stewardship of the U.S. living marine resources and their habitat." The agency's track record is erratic at best, "dangerous" and "damaging" if you were to ask a commercial fisherman. The IRS may not be popular with the general public, but to fishermen, NMFS is way worse.

NMFS operates through a number of regional councils. Montauk is part of the Mid-Atlantic Council which covers New York down to North Carolina while Rhode Island and Massachusetts landed in the New England Council. It's not hard to see why there might be problems. Two boats fishing side by side, but the one from Montauk is subject to stricter limits than the one from Block Island only fifteen miles away. Go figure. A one-year stint as President of the Montauk Boatman's Association is now likely to include trips to meetings in Maine or Virginia with a stop in Washington, D.C., along the way.

I doubt Ralph Pitts or any of the captains we interviewed at the Tipperary paid much attention to their local congressman. It wasn't long after the Magnuson Act was passed that every professional fisherman not only knew who their congressman was but probably had his office on speed dial.

Approximately 30 giant bluefin tuna after the last day of the 1956 U. S. Atlantic Tuna Tournament. White sign designated biggest fish, 758 lbs. caught by Robert Akin III (black slacks) and to his right mate Harry Clemenz, and Capt. Jim Sarno. All fish were trucked to a cat food factory the next morning. ©Montauk Library. Akin Collection

SP$RT FISHING

The best things in life are free,
but you can give them to the birds and bees,
I need money, that's what I want.

BERRY GORDY

COMMERCIAL FISHERMEN EARN A LIVING SELLING FISH. Sportfishermen go out to enjoy the experience of being on the water and maybe the excitement of "fighting" a big fish. In 1945, the International Game Fish Association published comprehensive guidelines for sportfishing. Their stated purpose: "To set and maintain the highest standards of ethics and create rules accordingly." When the Montauk Yacht Club held its annual Decathlon tournament, these rules (and ethics) were strictly applied. For example, if a boat carried a harpoon it might use to stick a swordfish, it was prohibited from entering the competition. Boat owners and anglers were proud of the designation "sportsman."

But it wasn't too many years after the Beatles were singing "I need money," and the Hollywood blockbuster *Wall Street* was preaching "Greed is good," that an age-old human virus began to infect the sportfishing crowd. Prices of seafood, especially tuna, exploded as people started eating more fish. The sushi craze was just beginning to ramp up, and tuna was the number one choice on the menu. The notion that you could make money sportfishing was embraced seemingly unchallenged.

This one account exemplifies how fast things change: Eighty boats, at least twenty from Montauk, competed in the 1956 Atlantic Tuna Tournament held at Point Judith, Rhode Island. In three days they landed nearly fifty giant bluefins. The fish were kept dockside in unrefrigerated trucks so pictures could be taken after the last day. The fourth day the trucks delivered the decomposing tuna to a cat food factory. Using a conservative calculation, twenty-five years later those fish would be worth over a million dollars.

As prices and demand increased in the 1980's, buyers became more sophisticated. The Japanese were willing to pay the highest prices, but they were also the most demanding. So much so that one Japanese wholesaler flew Tommy Edwards, a key employee at Carl Darenberg's Montauk Marine Basin, over to Tokyo so he could be educated in how to evaluate the quality of tuna. When a big tuna was weighed in, Tommy would take a core sample and test it for fat content. If it met certain criteria, the fish was put in a crate of ice, trucked to JFK, and flown overnight to Japan's Tsukiji Fish Market. A tuna caught Monday off Montauk could be sold Tuesday in Tokyo. Tommy remembers paying up to thirty dollar a pound for a good fish.

That a five-hundred-pound fish might be worth over ten thousand dollars caused problems everywhere. Charter boat customers started arguing with captains over who owned the catch. Some private boat owners also got into the game.

This was completely contrary to the spirit of sportfishing. Frank Tuma: *People used to fish for fun or a fish to take home. I don't think anyone came to Montauk with the thought of catching a load of fish and selling it. But that's the concept we have today, and that's what's hurting the industry. People who come today are so money conscious that it's hard for me to see anybody getting back to really going out there for fun. You don't have people who come to Montauk to fish for the fun of it. People like Billy Carpenter, Al Whisnant, Russ MacGrotty, and Bob Akin.*

I talked to a party this summer who has a fifty-five-foot Bertram, and he's questioning whether to go out fishing because the price of tuna is down. Look, you go out to have fun, but when you start making a business out of it … the days of real sportfishing, I don't think you will ever see that again. Everything changes of course. Nothing is forever.

I ran into the same mentality when I dropped by the Montauk Marine Basin in the mid-'90s. Word was out that some giants were showing up offshore, so I asked if a particular boat was open for a charter. A guy overheard and reminded me that the quota had been filled and the season was already closed. I told him that I didn't intend to keep the fish, but if I was lucky enough to hook a fish, I intended to release it. His answer: "Why would you want to do that?"

To be fair, even the old-time "ethical" sportfishing purists (this includes me and my family) had their faults. In retrospect, egregious faults. When boats brought in dozens of school tuna, hardly anyone wanted them. The fish were routinely kicked off the dock to sit on the bottom like aquatic compost. There was very little market even for the giant bluefins. White marlin were rarely released. Occasionally, someone would have one smoked, but most were towed out and cut loose the next day, minus the bill. The bills were collected as trophies. It was all part of sportfishing, or "recreational" fishing, as derived from the Latin meaning "refresh oneself by some amusement." And while a nice day on the water can certainly be restorative, let's not forget that the fish is not feeling restored nor is she amused.

No doubt an angler's reward is a higher priority (to him) than anything the fish might be experiencing. Bragging rights and ego were onboard in the old days just as they are today. It's understandable and adds to the fun. Fishing would be nothing without fish stories. But like every competition, no matter how restrained, things can get out of hand.

Even Ernest Hemingway, not known for his empathy, felt the need to comment on this in his introduction for Kip Farrington's 1937 book, *Atlantic Game Fishing*: "The sport is about due for a good house cleaning if it is to continue as a sport. If it is to be merely a contest of egos on who can produce the largest fish at the dock by any means, then let it become ridiculous as soon as possible." Again, that was Hemingway in 1937!

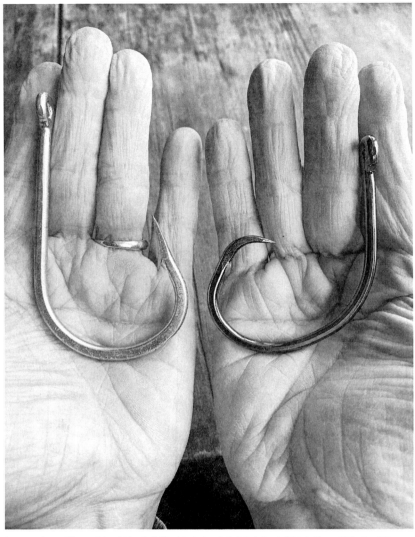

A comparison of the traditional J-hook (left) with the less lethal circle hook (right). Photo ©Monika Akin

A VERY GOOD THING

The event was a true success. All sharks released, 31 makos!!!
Amazing.

Joe Gaviola

FISHERMEN, BOTH SPORT AND COMMERCIAL, ARE NOT AN UNCARING bunch. By the turn of this century, the decline in fish stocks was an unavoidable reality. And while bureaucratic regulations attempted to put the brakes on the slide, a few enlightened souls were looking for something they could do one-on-one with the fish. The answer was part practical and part attitudinal.

Billfish such as marlin (white, blue, striped, and black) and sailfish are great fun to catch but make lousy eating. Yes, some will argue that a smoked white marlin is delicious, but one smoked marlin makes a lot of pate. Many anglers released these fish once they had been brought to the boat, but too often the fish would be hooked in the stomach (gut hooked) or the throat. These fish were unlikely to survive even if released. No one was happy when this happened. If a fish was hooked in the corner of the mouth, it had a much better chance to live.

The willingness to catch and release fish had grown steadily since the early days of sportfishing. Even so, fishermen were too often stung by the sight of a gut-hooked fish being reeled to the boat with a wine-red cloud of blood streaming from his gills. By the end of the twentieth century, sport anglers wanted to do the right thing but didn't see any options. Help came from an unlikely source.

In the early 1990s, long-range fishermen out of San Diego began experimenting with a different kind of hook while chunking for southern bluefin tuna. Instead of the traditional J-shaped hook, they began using a hook where the point was turned inward forming a three-quarters closed circle. The thought was the hook would not catch in the fish's gut or throat but rather in the corner of the jaw. Ironically, these tuna fishermen were not concerned about mortality. They just wanted a hook that was more effective. And it worked.

By the 1990s the sportfishing crowd had discovered the wildly plentiful quantity of sailfish and marlin along the Central American west coast. A good day fishing for sailfish off Florida might amount to a release of five fish. In Costa Rica, Panama, and Guatemala the numbers were closer to forty. And no one wanted to kill even one of these animals.

About the same time, fishermen working the waters off the North Carolina coast in the winter months discovered a concentration of giant bluefin tuna. Veteran guide Peter B. Wright (Peter was a mate on a boat at the Deep Sea Club in the '60s) and angler Skip Walton began using circle hooks as part of their efforts to tag and release bluefins that scientists had implanted with satellite tracking tags. This was expensive work and survival of the fish was critical.

The program worked and Wright got word out to his friend Tim Choate, owner of Pacific Fins, one of Guatemala's top fishing camps. Choate, encouraged by Captain Ron Hamlin, encouraged circle hooks to be used on all his charter boats. The result: they caught more fish, and the survival rate skyrocketed. Word spread.

But what about Montauk? There were no sailfish to release, and by 2000 very few white marlin were even being seen. Shark fishing had become the rage. Several marinas had begun sponsoring shark tournaments with surprisingly big prize money. Unfortunately, these tournaments were all "kill" tournaments. No one had thought much about releasing sharks. The questionable ethics of this did not go unnoticed by a few dedicated environmentalists. But change, when it finally arrived, came about through a sort of odd couple union.

For years, Sag Harbor artist April Gornick and Montauk's own Rav Freidel had vigorously protested local shark tournaments. Standing by the side of the road waving signs, they succeeded only to aggravate the fishermen. But after a cautious conversation with Joe Gaviola, winner of the previous three tournaments, the unlikely trio agreed to reach out to Carl Darenberg (son of the Carl Darenberg interviewed at the Tipperary). Carl sponsored one of the biggest shark tournaments and was a very respected member of the Montauk fishing community. Even better, Carl was at heart an old-school sportsman.

Unknown to the Freidel/Gornick/Gaviola trio, a few captains had already complained to Carl about the unnecessary toll on sharks that were the result of the tournaments. In 2013, knowing he had support from both fishermen and environmentalists, Carl scheduled an all-release competition in addition to his established event. Both tournaments specified circle hooks. The new competition was more than a success. Gaviola, deservedly delighted with the results, put it this way: "The event was a true success. All sharks released — 31 Makos!!! Amazing! — satellite tags in place and the fishing and enthusiasm was phenomenal."

Still not satisfied, Rav Freidel continued to fight for the sharks. He took the case to Albany. With unwavering effort he got the state law changed to mandate circle hooks for shark fishing in New York waters. On to Washington, and the federal government followed suit. This was one very good thing for the fish as well as the fishermen.

Some of the author's trophies from competitions in Montauk, Cape Hatteras, and Bimini. ©Akin Collection

AND NOW

Fishermen are an unrelenting lot. At the most elite level
of the sport, they will do anything, go anywhere,
and spend any amount of money to catch fish.

BILL AKIN

TODAY THERE IS SOME GOOD NEWS FOR MONTAUK FISHERMEN, BUT not much. Regulations have helped somewhat to restore swordfish stocks, but sportfishing for swordfish is limited to nights with glow sticks and deep baits in the canyons eighty miles offshore. I am unaware of any swordfish in the 250-pound range put on the dock in the last several years.

Even after being decimated in the late 1950s and '60s, the Butterfish Hole has shown an amazing capacity to recover, if only for brief periods. In the early 1990s charter boats saw more fish returning to this traditional area. Local trawlers were doing better as well. But it didn't last. About that time New England's most productive fishing grounds, Georges Banks, were closed due to overfishing. Numerous commercial boats redirected their efforts south to the Butterfish Hole. Unable to sustain the added pressure, once more the stock collapsed.

And again, as recently as 2019 there were some positive signs. Capt. Ricky Etzel on the *Breakaway* has told me there was a decent run of bluefin in the area and that whiting and ling were plentiful on the bottom. Even large schools of menhaden, aka bunkers, have begun to reappear after successful efforts by environmentalists to curtail commercial overfishing in the Chesapeake Bay. We can only hope these trends last.

Meanwhile, restrictions on the number, size, and season for tuna have managed to maintain some breeding stock, but the total biomass of Atlantic bluefin in 2015 was 18% of 1950 and 45% of 1974 according to the 2017 stock report by the International Convention for the Conservation of Atlantic Tuna. Last year there were no giant bluefins brought in to Montauk.

Meanwhile, inshore striped bass and fluke fishing is good, but regulations characterized by captains as "crazy," "arbitrary," "unfair," "f--ked up," "asinine," "ludicrous," "ridiculous," or simply "stupid" are a constant headache.

The number of full-time, full-size charter boats has dwindled in recent years. A few captains, such as Barry Kohlus (*Venture II*), Dave Kohlus (*Adah-K*), Ricky Etzel (*Breakaway*), Skip Rudolph (*Adios*), and others somehow manage to hang on. But it's not easy. Not only must they deal with the above-mentioned tangle of regulations as well as fewer big-game fish such as marlin, swordfish, and tuna, but their competition now includes a mish-mash of private vessels that occasionally charter and the new "mosquito fleet" of small center-console inshore fly fishing boats that target striped bass and false albacore.

Shark fishing is the mainstay for the offshore charter business, and there are still a number of shark tournaments every year. As mentioned before, circle hooks are mandated for these tournaments, but support for 100% release tournaments has sadly evaporated.

Montauk's general public continues to be well served by a number of party boats including three Viking vessels, the *Lazy Bones*, *Marlin II*, and *Miss Montauk*. The Viking operation also runs a New London and Block Island ferry service, night cruises, and one commercial boat. The fleet now consists of seven vessels.

Fishermen today, with few exceptions, are far more responsible than in the past. Circle hooks improve the chances that a released fish will survive. They are not only mandated for sharks but are also well accepted among tuna anglers. Striped bass fishermen are also using circle hooks and often keep fewer fish than regulations would permit.

Specific commercial fisheries have been both successful and responsible by targeting particular species. Montauk boats operating deep-water longlines for golden tilefish have had decades of profitable seasons while traditional bottom trawlers operate under strict, but wildly imperfect, regulations. No doubt pelagic longline vessels are subject to the most extreme regulatory practice as they are now required to carry cameras to monitor their catch.

The fish have also gained some allies. In addition to regulations, there are now hundreds of fisheries conservation organizations operating locally, regionally, and internationally. The majority of these non-profit institutions were founded and managed by fishermen themselves. But they face many serious problems. Open-ocean environmental management is extremely difficult, and relies on inexact science resulting in countless controversial decisions. Regional and national conflicts are numerous and passionately contested.

The International Commission for the Conservation of Atlantic Tunas (ICCAT) is also responsible for the conservation of tuna-like species in the Atlantic Ocean. Annual meetings attract envoys from forty-nine countries. Quotas are set to protect tuna and other pelagic fish, but these quotas will also impact the lives of commercial fishermen worldwide. As such, politics at the highest, nastiest level can come into play. In backroom meetings prior to one annual ICCAT meeting, Japan threatened to cancel a huge government loan agreement with an African nation if it did not agree to vote in favor of Japan's request to expand the annual bluefin quota.

In the U.S., the Marine Fish Conservation Network is a coalition of thirty conservation groups focused primarily on upholding and enforcing existing laws such as the Magnuson-Stevens Act.

Looking ahead, perhaps the most important development for the future of fishing is the multitude of scientists and researchers now spread across the world studying fish and the marine ecosystems that sustain them. Fisheries are a tapestry of predator-prey relationships. If you pull too hard on one or another thread, the fabric begins to come apart. Human beings have become super predators yanking on many sides, but without yet understanding how all the strands fit together. The work of these research professionals is critical. I like to think of them all as descendants of Jacques Cousteau, one of my boyhood heroes.

Getting the word out to the public is also important. Satellite tags on great white sharks and bluefin tuna now transmit data on migration patterns and breeding grounds. In some cases their progress can even be followed on a home computer. A few years ago, schoolchildren in Montauk were given the opportunity to name a thresher shark that was caught, tagged, and released during the Montauk Marine Basin shark tournament. They chose *Big Kahuna*. The whole class tracked her for a year.

The fish and the ocean need all the help they can get. Fishermen are an unrelenting lot. At the most elite level of the sport, they will do anything, go anywhere, and spend any amount of money to catch fish. What goes on today is just a high-dollar extension of what Maytag, Cassulo, Phipps, and others were doing back in the 1960s.

Over a hundred years ago, sportsman and author Zane Grey conceived the mothership method of fishing. With a mothership, a smaller "fish boat" is towed by, or carried aboard, a much larger vessel, usually a luxury yacht. The aim was to reach locations that would be out of range for smaller craft. As a consequence, I doubt there are any reefs, seamounts, or exotic islands left in the world that have not been fished.

Such adventures don't come cheap. Anyone chartering a mothership operation is basically renting two boats with two full crews, and there are no one-day charters. Nevertheless, it is an exceptional experience.

In '93 I was lucky to get a last-minute invite to join three friends on a trip to Australia's Great Barrier Reef. Someone had cancelled his trip and forfeited half of the cost. We would be fishing for black marlin, one of the biggest game fish in the world, sometimes weighing over a thousand pounds. We were a 100% release charter.

Our mothership was a 110-foot yacht anchored just inside the barrier reef but forty miles offshore. Each morning breakfast was served on the fantail at a comfortable hour, and then we stepped aboard the 43-foot "fish boat" to head out. Ten minutes later, we passed through one of the many cuts in the huge reef and the baits went into the indigo blue water of the Coral Sea. All that week, whether we trolled twenty miles north or south, the mothership, alerted by radio, followed us, and was always there just inside the reef to meet us at the end of the day. I remember getting back the first afternoon and being greeted by the steward: "Dinner is rack of lamb. Would you like your cocktail before or after you shower?" Seven days later a seaplane pulled alongside to fly us back to Cairns and reality.

That was twenty-seven years ago, and aside from two days fishing from an outboard-powered panga in Mexico, it was my final outing. Occasionally I'll take a rod down to the beach in Montauk and cast for bass, but I'm not very good at it. My father sold our boat sometime in the 1970s, and from then until the Australia trip I hitched rides with friends on other boats. St. Thomas for blue marlin, Costa Rica for sailfish and marlin, and finally Bimini in the early '80s for the last years of a dwindling bluefin tuna migration.

I am often asked why I stopped. I had been fishing since I was five years old and had caught several white marlin, sailfish, blue marlin, swordfish, and one giant bluefin tuna before I could legally drive a car. Furthermore, I still love the ocean: the distinctive smells from inshore to offshore, the infinite shades of blue and green, how light changes hour to hour as the breeze stiffens in the afternoon, the wildlife — sea birds, turtles, whales, dolphins — but mostly the unceasing roll of gentle swells from some far off storm, uninterrupted from horizon to horizon, hour after hour, day after day, never the same.

I suppose there are many reasons why I have chosen to step away, the most obvious being cost. Big-game fishing has become ridiculously expensive. But I know there is more to it than that. Simply put, it is a different ocean, and I am a different person. No doubt I was an exceptionally lucky kid to have had the chance to do what I did and to count as my friends so many hard working professionals. But perhaps it's because I started at such an early age that now, given these years away from the water, I see a different picture. Today I find it impossible to separate what's happening out on the ocean from the blind obliteration of wild creatures happening everyday on dry land. And just like there are far fewer fish, I am aware that there are far fewer songbirds each summer dawn. Fewer wildflowers, fewer butterflies. I find myself rooting for the wild world to hang in there.

I still treasure my memories of days on the ocean with my father, mother, and brother, but I can no longer view the pictures of my prize-winning fish or my collection of trophies without hearing Hemingway's cautionary words: *Anglers have a way of romanticizing their battles with fish and forgetting that the fish has a hook in his mouth, his gullet, or his belly and that his gameness is really the extreme of panic in which he runs, leaps, and pulls to get away until he dies.*

Much of Montauk's fishing history hangs on the walls of a few bars and restaurants. This one in the Shagwong Tavern in downtown Montauk.

EPILOGUE

No more than a brief shining moment.

BILL AKIN

IT IS ONLY IF YOU GO DOWN TO THE DOCKS IN THE FIRST HOUR OR SO after sunrise that you can smell it. Before too many cars have arrived, and before the boats have fired up, the scent is both clean and rich. It rises from the water as it washes against the bulkheads and pilings covered with algae and barnacles.

I am rarely at the docks at that early hour these days, but I know the scent is there just a short drive away. Although it is a calm scent, it is full of anticipation, excitement, and hope for a good day out on the ocean.

Fishing is not only an important part of our local economy, it was, and still is, woven into Montauk life. Is fishing better or worse these days? The long trend is discouraging, but there are bright spots. Anglers and crews struggle with regulations, but still manage to catch striped bass, fluke, sharks, big-eye, yellow-fin, and even an occasional bluefin tuna. High-powered boats charge eighty miles offshore to the canyon hoping for a chance at a marlin or a deep-water night strike from a swordfish. Closer to shore, swordfish and marlin are nearly non-existent. And although the charter boat fleet has dropped from its peak, every summer day there are still second and third-generation Montauk captains who guide their customers around Shagwong Point and out past the lighthouse. The annual Blessing of the Fleet in June continues to be an important local celebration.

In Montauk's downtown Shagwong Tavern, Gosman's Lookout Bar, and in the harbor's Montauk Market, there is a photographic record hanging on the walls. Carl Darenberg, Ralph and Gus Pitts, Frank and Bob Tuma, George and John Potts, Harry Clemenz, and many others are all up there somewhere. The pictures serve mostly to add character or atmosphere. No one pays much attention. Tourists coming in from a day on the beach might consider these black and whites quaint, charming, almost old-world. They hang there as reminders of a past that has retreated into its own hermetically sealed world. But for those who searched hours from a mast-head for the sickle fins of a swordfish, or gazed across acres of shimmering tuna just below the surface, or fought giant bluefins less than a mile off the Rhode Island beaches, for these lucky few, it will always be real.

Now, as the decades have stumbled by, events have forced me to accept that what we witnessed is lost to history:

In 1988, Carl Fisher's Star Island Club casino and home to the Deep Sea Club was destroyed by fire.

In 2015 the IGFA museum of sportfishing, unable to attract enough visitors in South Florida, was moved from Dania Beach to Springfield, Missouri, home of its new owner, Bass Pro Shops. There are no marlin in the Mississippi River.

A Japanese buyer paid $3.1 million for a single bluefin tuna in 2019.

On January 13, 2006, the Compleat Angler Inn in Bimini burned to the ground. The dancing, drinking, and great times were only the icing. Also lost were the dark varnished walls covered with fishing history, a library where Hemingway wrote *To Have and Have Not,* and the joyful mix of locals, boat owners, and crews. The Compleat Angler was an emotional homeport for generations of sportfishermen from Cape Cod to Key West.

And finally, in 2018 a New York-based venture capital group acquired the historic Montauk Yacht Club, changed the name to Gurney's Star Island Resort, and stripped the walls of pictures recalling the club's distinguished past.

Today Montauk is most famous for surfing, nightclubs, parties, a variety of Pepperidge Farm chocolate chip cookies, and beer.

When anglers traveled from all over the world to fish in Montauk, no one could have foreseen this future. The fishing we have today is what it is. And as exciting as it was, Montauk's golden age of sportfishing is now only history, no more than a brief shining moment. But for those — most no longer with us — who lived it, our memories will never fade. So be it. Fish have tails. Time moves on.

Entrance to The Compleat Angler in Bimini prior to 2006 fire which destroyed the entire structure.
©Wikipedia.org

Robert Akin Jr. ©W.D. Akin. Dave Edwardes Collection

AFTERWORD

Robert M. Akin, Jr., "The Old Man"

There is a naval tradition that the captain of a ship be known as "The Old Man." It is a title of respect, and not every senior officer is so recognized. I can't recall precisely when my father picked up the designation, but a good guess would be sometime around when our family's sportfishing boat, the *Nika*, was launched in 1952. Dad was a big fan of the Navy, and although his one blind eye prevented him from ever serving, he considered it a great privilege to have been invited as an industrial observer aboard the *USS Panamint* as part of Operation Crossroads to witness the Bikini atom bomb tests in 1946.

Soon after returning from Bikini, whether it was from our home in Westchester or the summer house in Westhampton, my father began driving the family's wooden station wagon to Montauk to go fishing. Montauk was a skeleton of the town it is today. There were only a few charter boats for hire, and my dad soon became well acquainted with the local captains including Ralph Pitts and Frank Tuma. After his own boat was launched and our family moved to Montauk for summers in 1953, Dad treasured his friendships with these Montauk pioneers. These captains were as much his heroes as any of the admirals he met during Operation Crossroads.

Even as a child, whether it was fishing in the Hudson River near where he was born in Ossining, NY, or on Cape Cod in South Yarmouth where his family spent summers, he had always lived near water. As a young boy he would travel alone from Ossining to New York City by ferry and then transfer to another for an overnight trip through Long Island Sound, past Montauk, and out to the Cape. Today this sounds like an adventure, but not so to my father, or to his family who traced their heritage back to Nantucket whalers.

Whether he was aware of it or not, I suspect it was this family legacy as much as his reverence for the Navy as to why he willingly embraced "The Old Man" moniker. But for whatever reason, it stuck with him. Even now my nieces and nephew only refer to him as "The Old Man," or just the OM. At the factory where he worked for sixty-five years, rising to Chairman of the Board, nearly everyone, including veteran shop floor supervisors, engineers, officers, and even the firm's attorney adopted the title.

You might think that with such a family history and esteemed title, The Old Man would have been a reserved, buttoned-up kind of gentleman. Actually, he might have even thought so himself. But there was too much of the mad scientist in the man for the picture to fit.

Robert M. Akin, Jr. was a wildly talented self-taught electrical engineer. An early acceptance to Harvard was withdrawn after a disciplinary issue at the Morristown Academy landed him in trouble. Somehow he had managed to wire the copper piping throughout the school to allow coded messages to be shared with other students — sort of a pioneer internet, or inter-pipe. The school ignored his gift and dismissed him.

Dad was born in 1904, the same year his father had founded a small wire company, Hudson Wire, in Ossining. He grew up obsessed with electricity, a fascination the population of Ossining became suddenly aware of one summer afternoon. Seems the young Akin boy and a friend had snuck off with a stolen case of dynamite, connected it to a charger, and strung two very lengthy wires up a hill above the village to the friend's house where they asked the father if he knew how to twist them together. As a result of the explosion, young Akin spent a good part of the next year doing odd jobs to pay off what the family spent reimbursing neighbors and shop owners for a host of shattered windows.

As he grew older, my father applied his talents more constructively. Staying with electricity, he built the first television in New York State (it sits on a shelf in my relatives' Montauk house). He also invented the method for electroplating silver onto copper wire. This doesn't sound like such a great accomplishment until you consider that only silver can withstand the heat required to insulate copper wire with what was then the newly invented Teflon insulation product. And Teflon was the required insulation for all wiring in military aircraft, missiles, and later, satellites.

The Nika was built for Robert Akin Jr. by South Bay Boatworks, Patchogue, NY. In 1952. ©Akin Collection

My mother, brother, and I were not immune to dad's obsession. He had always been an amateur, or ham, radio operator. Lots of people shared this hobby (and still do) without causing any issues. But not The Old Man. He was never satisfied with his radio broadcast capabilities, and his go-to option for juicing performance levels involved antennas. Not just bigger versions of the ones you would see on roof tops. Dad's improvisations involved stringing various length wires from one tree to another. Or from a chimney to a tree. Or from a tree to a telephone pole he paid to have installed in our backyard. None of these trees or poles were close to each other. Setting it up involved tree companies, a series of pulleys, extension saws, and lots of help from cheap labor, which meant me. (My brother, having reached driving age, was somehow never around.) Our yard back in Sleepy Hollow had so many wires strung from one place to another, the local birds probably considered it a no-fly zone.

Inside the house, dad kept his radio operation in the basement. I have none of my father's electrical aptitude, so I have no idea how it happened, but one night when he was talking away downstairs, my mother was caught off guard when she opened her new electric oven and heard her husband's voice emanating from the roast.

While my father was best known for his electrical inventions and adventures, he had other eccentricities. The best you could say about how he chose to dress was that it was casual. But even that doesn't cover it. Was he a slob? Not really, but my wife knew him for the last few years of his life and swears she never saw him in a shirt that didn't have a stain on it. Bottom line, he really didn't care.

At the factory, even when he was supposed to be in his office doing what presidents do, he would frequently disappear down to the machine shop where one of his oldest friends was the supervisor. Dad was a hands-on guy, and if there was something he could help with, he was all in.

I can't say what that day's project was, but somehow dad must have spent time sitting on whatever was nearest to the project, probably a spare battery. An hour or two later at lunch in a nearby club, he was helping himself to a sandwich buffet when the company treasurer approached him suggesting he take a seat. I'm sure all was in order when he left home that morning, but an hour after his stint in the machine shop, the back side of his suit pants had disintegrated. No doubt battery acid. He took his seat, finished lunch, tied his coat around his waist and went back to the office.

For much of the first half of the twentieth century America was booming, and dad was a big fan of industry. By the 1950s, damage to the environment was just beginning to show, but very few people were paying attention. Having witnessed the first Bikini bomb tests in July of 1946, my father was a huge advocate for nuclear energy. He downplayed the risks even in later years when the dangers of nuclear energy were better understood. And maybe his attitude was understandable given that he survived for decades after having walked on the decks of bombed-out decommissioned Navy ships one day after the bomb blast. He liked to tell how he rolled out of his bunk the next day, picked up his shoes off a stack of undeveloped old-fashioned photography plates, and found a perfectly developed image of his left shoe. Like, if I'm still here, how bad can this stuff be?

Dad was extremely proud of his Bikini adventure. He had become friendly with some top Navy people including Admirals George Blandy and Chester Nimitz, Jr. Both would later visit us in Montauk. His enthusiasm is reflected in a letter he sent me from Bikini. I have it framed in my living room along with the stamped and postmarked envelope from Bikini Atoll, certainly one of the last posts from that ill-fated island.

1 July, 46

Dear Bill

While you are only twenty months old at this time, someday you will be old enough to read this letter.

Today or tomorrow we will set off the fourth atomic bomb ever exploded. I hope this will be the last time atomic bombs are ever used to destroy property or things that men have spent many hours of hard work to plan and build, Someday you will fly out to this island of Bikini in a plane and instead of two weeks to arrive you will make it in two hours powered by the same energy and fuel that will destroy all these beautiful ships today. When you grow up the whole world will be much closer together and you will never need to leave your family for two or three months.

Be a good boy for now.

Your Dad

After the war my father took over management of the family business from his father. By then the firm had grown to include four factories spread out from Connecticut to Michigan. Still Montauk, and his fishing friends, were never far from his mind. From 1953 to '55 our family rented summer houses in Montauk from the Tuma family, and then in 1956 my father bought a house. Actually, three houses.

Built in 1927 as the private residence for Montauk (and Miami Beach) developer Carl Fisher, the house had sat unoccupied since the military evacuated after WWII. The former officers' quarters, annex/garage, and caretaker's cottage included sixteen bedrooms. And though this was thirteen more than our family of four required, between friends and business customers, most of the rooms were occupied weekends July through October.

In the '50s and '60s Long Island was headquarters for several aerospace companies. And aerospace was the end use for much of the products the family wire company manufactured. Executives and buyers from these companies and their suppliers were more than happy to accept an invitation for a weekend in Montauk that included all accommodations, meals, refreshments, and a couple of days fishing. The Montauk trips were so popular that many weekends our one boat could not handle everyone. My father chartered his old friends, Ralph Pitts, Walter Droebecker, Frank Tuma, and others to take out the overflow.

The house, or weekend hotel, required help to manage the rooms and prepare most of the meals, but my father insisted on making breakfast. As he was not a heavy drinker, or "party animal," he was always the first to retire at night and first up in the morning. And while fishing was supposed to be what the weekends were all about, unlike The Old Man, not everyone was full of enthusiasm at 6 AM.

The author and father with his first swordfish, 1958. ©Montauk Library. Akin Collection

One particularly unfortunate guest had continued the evening party by heading downtown. Just after dawn the next morning, his overnight companion dropped him off at the end of the driveway. The Old Man, oblivious to the situation, was delighted to see someone who he thought was enjoying the morning and ready to head out for the day. The customer was not about to explain himself to his host. Breakfast was followed by a ride down to the boat, and a full day on the water mostly spent unconscious on a bunk in the cabin. Years later my father heard the full story. His response was typical: "He was invited out here to go fishing, and that's damn well what he was going to do."

Most days when boats returned from fishing, owners and crews mingled on the dock at the Montauk Yacht Club. My father, the club's Vice Commodore, was always most comfortable talking with the captains and mates. Soon after acquiring the Fisher house, his friendship with these "professionals" resulted in an annual "crews only" cocktail party up at the house. Entertainment included a skeet shooting contest and a 9-iron competition from the backyard to a not-so-well-maintained golf green in a hollow well below the house. (A multitude of Montauk children have grown up knowing the place as Akin's Hill, the best sleigh riding in Montauk.)

As Montauk's reputation for big-game fishing began to flourish in the late '50s, The Old Man wanted to encourage his friends in the charter business to consider using the rod-and-reel method to catch swordfish. But swordfish were a valuable commodity and harpooning was the most reliable way to put a fish in the boat. Nevertheless, my father was convinced that the charter business would benefit if more customers thought they had a chance to go after what was then the most prized of all game fish. To help promote rod-and-reel fishing for swordfish, my father had small plaques made up for any captain who successfully landed a swordfish using rod and reel. He awarded these each year at the annual Montauk Boatman's Association dinners. The awards were very much appreciated, but more important, the charter fleet began booking a number of customers interested primarily in catching a swordfish. In 1958 the charter fleet landed forty-nine swordfish on rod and reel.

Businessman, Navy ambassador, Yacht Club commodore, electrical wizard (he received the David Sarnoff Award for exceptional contributions to electronics), and family man, my father was all of these. But at heart, The Old Man was an old salt. Nothing proves this more than what happened one day when we were anchored chumming for giant tuna and I caught a good-size codfish while bottom fishing for bait.

We had two customers on board that day, and neither was feeling well. Nevertheless, my father could not resist an opportunity to have some of what he considered fun. The cod, having been brought up from the bottom, was bloated from the pressure differential. This caused a sack of row to expel from the cod's belly. I guess this was considered a delicacy on Cape Cod when dad was a child growing up, so he squeezed out a handful, and without hesitating, gulped it down. He threw the cod in the water where it swam away. Both guests rushed to the stern depositing their breakfasts over the side.

The Old Man died of a heart attack at age 85, just one week after finalizing the contract to sell the company his father founded and where he worked for sixty-five years including the day he passed away. It was September 22, 1989. My mother was bedridden with severe dementia, so my father had made it a habit to watch the evening news by her bedside holding her hand. That night was no different. The news was all about Hurricane Hugo as it was slamming into the South Carolina coast. Winds had reached Category 5. A raging ocean was washing over barrier islands. People were frantically evacuating. The Old Man was at peace.

ACKNOWLEDGMENTS

WHEN I DISCOVERED THE TRANSCRIPT OF THE INTERVIEWS JOE Gaviola and I had recorded back in 1994, I realized that I was now at an age similar to that of the veteran captains we had taped. Perhaps it was this awareness of time that spurred me on to write this book. I soon realized that this doesn't happen without a whole lot of help from several friends and professionals. So, much thanks to:

The Montauk Library and archivist Maura Feeney for providing me access to the historical photo archives from the Edwardes Collection, Al Sari Collection, and Clemenz Collection, and also for letting me hear the digitized version of the original tapes. Also Robin Strong for having the foresight to have the tapes transcribed.

Tom Clavin, author and editor, for encouragement and guidance that can only come from a professional.

Jason Fairchild, Art Director and technical wiz at The Truesdale Group in Boston for his insight, patience, and enthusiasm. And Todd Trusdale for helping me understand how modern publishing worked.

Capt. Ricky Etzel who took me through page by page to correct what I had gotten wrong.

Debbie Tuma, daughter of Capt. Bob Tuma, for straightening me out on the Tuma family history.

Capt. Barry Kohlus for refreshing my memory and identifying faces I had never known.

Pam Lyons, Rob Kramer, and Tim Choate from Wild Oceans for providing guidance about the state of current fisheries, and some history on circle hooks.

Tom Edwardes, son of photographer Dave Edwardes, and someone who managed the tuna evaluations at the Montauk Marine Basin, as well as Mark Jarboe and Courtney Darenberg at the Marine Basin.

Jane Bimson at the East Hampton Star who was able to find background material that was not available in public archives.

My niece, Suzy Akin, for helping me with a number of grammar questions as well as a detailed final proofread. It's reassuring to know that someone in our family paid attention in school.

Over the course of finalizing the manuscript, I relied on several friends who helped me clarify what did not make sense to non-fishermen, as well as some very insightful comments on structure. Thanks go to: Andrew Harris, Jay Fruin, Roseanne and Ed Braun, Richard Kahn, Bob Stern, and Elaine Peterson.

My wife, Monika, who is the epitome of a non-fishermen, but still had the patience to read through the manuscript as it progressed, and explain to me most directly what made no sense.

Both Jim Grimes (the Pitts family) and Michael Potts filled me in on important family histories.

Dave Marcley passed along his pictures of the old Viking Grill.

Finally, my dear and oldest friend, Harry MacGrotty. He and I are the same age. Harry fished on his father's boat, the *Tumult*, all through the 1950's and 60's, and was exceptionally fortunate to have had both Carl Darenberg and Buddy Merritt as captains. Our memories of the years at the Yacht Club and Deep Sea Club are nearly identical.